Slice of Life

Short Fiction Stories & Poems

Reema Agarwal

PARTRIDGE
A Penguin Random House Company

| ISBN: | Softcover | 978-1-4828-5060-4 |
| | eBook | 978-1-4828-5061-1 |

Print information available on the last page.

To order additional copies of this book, contact
Partridge India
000 800 10062 62
orders.india@partridgepublishing.com

www.partridgepublishing.com/india

Preface

This book is a collection of short narrative stories and some of my poems. If I have to say what a reader would find in the book, well they'll find my stories to be emotional and I am certain somewhere they will touch the reader's heart. My poems are a reflection of my own thoughts somewhere; they deal with emotions of freedom, life, death, love, anguish towards society, life after death and a lot more.

The book is a reflection of my experiences in life and I have tried to pen down all the emotions that we go through in life at some point or the other.

Contents

Enroute To Find God

Where there is a will there is a way

The year is 1974 and it is a cold wintry night in the small hilly town of Ranikhet. The weather forecast on the radio has said there'll be snowfall tonight. It was just 8 in the evening but the roads here were deserted and it seemed the whole town was either sleeping or dead. The only sound that came was of a lonely cricket and a bat. Palash was eagerly waiting for the dinner to get over and everyone to go to bed. He was getting restless. His mother asked what the matter with him is, and why is he in such a rush. But Palash couldn't for the moment let out the truth, so instead he just said that he's hungry and tired; and that's the reason he wants to finish dinner soon and hop off to bed. He was looking at his mother from the corner of his eyes and she seemed to believe his story. He heaved a sigh of relief.

Finally for Palash those agonizing moments came to a halt when it was 11 in the night and everyone was sound sleep in their rooms. He checked again and then came back to his room, took out his rucksack and checked it for all the essentials that he was going to need. Everything was in place. He went into the kitchen and stacked his brown bag with cookies, snacks, biscuits, apples, and then he filled himself a big bottle of water. He was ready now; he sneaked out of the back door because it had a self lock system and so on his way out he won't put any of his family members in danger. Not that there was any danger but still he wanted to be cautious.

He headed towards Chiku's house; Chiku was his partner in this trip and he was his best friend too. He reached his friend's house and he stood near Chiku's bedroom window and whistled three times. Palash was hoping that Chiku doesn't falls asleep. Chiku had absolutely no control over his sleep and that was worrying Palash a lot. But thankfully today Chiku was wide awake and he too was ready with his rucksack and essentials for the journey that lay ahead of both of them. He too came out of the back door. They both were consumed with excitement for their trip.

This was the first time in their life of seven years that they were travelling all alone and un-chaperoned. They were nervous and excited at the same time as to what lay ahead of them. They went to the bus depot and boarded a bus to Kedarnath. The man at the ticket window was half asleep and that's why he didn't notice that they were travelling all alone.

It took almost two hours for the bus to fill in and then they started their journey to Kedarnath. The motion of the bus and the winding roads made both of them instantly fall asleep. The distance between Ranikhet and Kedarnath was not much but the hills always made the distance seem more because of the treacherously winding roads. Palash woke up after half an hour or so of sleep; he was very curious and excited about this journey. He was filled with lots of hopes and deep down he was convinced that he would achieve his goal. He opened the window a little and peeked out; it was dark but he still could see distant lights somewhere on the hills they were passing through. He always used to wonder who lived in those solitary standing houses on the mountains. How was it even possible to build a house up there? But there was also a beautiful thing about those houses; they were so near or they seemed so near to the skies. As if people who lived there would just step out on the terrace, raise their hands and touch the sky. He always used to wonder that how beautiful that feeling would be. Those tiny houses up there on the mountains with those little yellow flickering lights have always piqued his imagination. He had this secret wish to live in a house like that. Palash remembered that his grandfather always says that journey is not just about going to a place you haven't seen but there's more to it. His grandfather used to say that journey is about knowing people, making friends, learning their language, knowing their life and maybe for a day but living their life with them is a true sense of a journey. According to him those things mattered more than sightseeing. Finding diversity and then bridging the gaps by our love should be the main aim of a true traveller. For him you can say you have seen the place only if you have known the lives of people who live there. Some things made sense to Palash and some were too much for his seven year old mind to fathom.

Somewhere thinking about the majestic mountains, those tiny houses with yellow lights travels and his grandfather

Palash slept again and he was woken up by the constant honking of the bus. Chiku was wide awake and he told Palash that they have reached Kedarnath. The bus didn't have many passengers, people stayed away from travelling in the night on the hills; and somewhere it was a boon to Palash and Chiku because people hardly noticed them. They got down and straightaway headed to the washroom they could find at the depot. It was a cold day with nail biting chilly breeze. They even heard people saying that this October of '74 is too cold and god knows what would happen in the coming months of winter.

Now the biggest question lay ahead of them, and that was how to reach the temple of Kedarnath. Chiku said that they should ask someone and then tell them that they will be shortly joined in by their parents. That idea seemed okay to Palash. He went to an old man who had a wrinkled face; he was sitting with a cup of tea in one hand and a cigarette in the other. He was making smoke rings in the air and he looked quiet disconnected and disillusioned from the place he was in. Palash had to shake him a little to make him listen to what he had to say. After what felt like ages to Palash the old man answered and directed them on how to reach Kedarnath temple. Before embarking on the trek to the temple they both bought tea for themselves; a luxury they could only afford when alone and also ate some cookies.

It was almost 8 in the morning when they started their trek to the temple. Both of them were too excited that they didn't realize that the trek was treacherous and one wrong step would just land them in big trouble. Palash realized that it was beautiful; those winding treks and the river down there, the surrounding majesty of the snow clapped mountains was too overwhelming and breathtaking. They passed many people; some were walking like them, while some chose to take ride on a mule. Some were old, some were young, but what was common or the binding factor in everyone was faith. They all were going up there on this treacherous trek because they had an unflinching faith in the man up there; they knew that somehow in just his presence he would make all their woes, their troubles seem trivial and maybe he will make them disappear too. But Palash wanted to take that man up there from here to his house in Ranikhet maybe just for a day but he wanted him to come to his house.

After a long and tiring trek to the temple, everyone finally reached. Palash and Chiku were so excited that they just dumped their bags with the shoes and ran inside the temple to meet him finally and that too in person. They screeched to halt; the temple priest was performing a puja and he signalled them to wait. He finished his puja and then he walked towards them and asked them where their parents are? Palash felt bad lying inside the temple premise but still he had to save himself; so he replied that they are coming and will be here anytime soon. He then asked the temple priest to take him to God. He told the priest that he very urgently wants to talk to God as he is the only one who can solve all his troubles. The priest was a little bewildered and he told Palash that he is right in front of God. He asked Palash to pray to him and he said God will definitely look into his matter and grant his wish. Palash and Chiku were a little apprehensive about this; but nevertheless they prayed and then came out. They both looked pensive. Palash was apprehensive of praying because he has always seen his grandmother to pray to same idol at home and it didn't make sense to his little mind as to why he has travelled so far to pray to the same idol. He was expecting a person named god to be here; someone who would listen to him and talk to him and would come with him to Ranikhet. But that didn't happen.

Palash and Chiku were too exhausted with the trek and the fact that the person named God is not here. They went at the backside of the temple sat there; they were now thinking hard where to find God. Palash was too sad with all this and he started to cry silently. He was so hopeful that he would meet God and then take him to his house. It was when Chiku was sitting dejectedly on a rock gazing at kids playing in the distance and Palash was silently crying that a man came and sat beside him. He wiped Palash's tears and asked him what is the matter with him; why is he crying?

Palash looked at the man sitting beside him. He was tall, very fair skinned and his eyes were like an ocean; they were so kind, compassionate and deep. To Palash he looked like a sage. He was wearing a dhoti and he had long hair. His voice was a melodious rhythm to ears and his words seemed like they were flowing out of his mouth in a mellifluous way. His whole persona to Palash was enchanting and enigmatic. Palash felt safe in his presence and thus he poured out his heart to him. He told him that his elder sister is sick; everyone says she has cancer and its one in a million chances that she would survive. Palash told that sage that every time he asks that when she will be fine, he is always told god knows. Everyone keeps saying that now it's god's will. He told the sage that this is the reason he wanted to find God and that he has once heard his grandmother refer to someone that god lives here in Kedarnath and that's the reason he has come here all the way from Ranikhet to find god and take him back to Ranikhet, so that he can cure his sister. He asked the sage to wait for a minute and then he ran to get his bag. He came back zipped open his bag and took out a piggy bank. He emptied that in front of the sage and he told him that he will give every dime in this piggy bank to god. He then took out a collection of batman comics and said that he will also give this to god; he said that's all he's got. He said he wishes that this much is okay with God and that he agrees to go with him and cure his sister. Palash told the sage that he loves his sister a lot; she is so beautiful and she has always been so caring for him and now when it's his turn to do something for her, he has failed because he is unable to find god. He started to cry again.

All this while the sage was quietly listening to Palash; his heart went out to him. He was thinking that he has seen people asking for things from god but never ever has he seen such selfless devotion and that too from a little seven year old boy. Just to please god he was ready to give up on his prized possessions and even his money. He wasn't even asking anything for himself, he just wanted his sister to be all fine and healthy again. He was deeply touched by this little boy's devotion. He kissed Palash on the forehead and told him to go back to his house because everyone would be worried about him. He told him to go back, as maybe his sister is fine now and she is missing him. Palash looked at him in complete disbelief. The sage said that maybe God changed his mind and finally he came to his house when Palash left last night. This made sense to Palash. He wiped his tears and yelled out to Chiku who was now playing in the distance with some kids he had befriended.

They both now were ready to go; something made Palash turn back and go to the sage. He was still there sitting on the rock. He went there and gave a tight hug to the sage and kissed him on the cheeks and thanked him for talking to him. Palash told him that he was a good man and that if at his house he meets God he would ask God to give a special gift to the sage. He said he was getting late and he needs to go. But before saying good bye he asked the sage what was his name. The sage smiled and replied that his friends called him Rudra and now that Palash is his friend, he too can call him Rudra. Palash extended his hand and said nice to meet you Rudra and then he took out a pen from his bag and wrote his number on Rudra's palms and asked him to call him. He waved a kiss to him and went ahead to résumé his journey back home. Rudra was smiling and he felt overwhelmed with Palash's faith in god. He knew he has made an exception today but he was happy with it; he absolutely had no regrets. He thought once in a while even gods can make an exception and surprise people.

Epilogue

The dust has finally settled over Palash's and Chiku's daredevil escapade to find god. It was a risky thing to do, to venture out like that. But everyone understood their feelings and eventually after being grounded for a month they were forgiven and now they are free as a bird. Palash is super happy because the mysterious man called god has cured his sister and now she is on the road to a speedy and a miraculous recovery. Palash is also eagerly awaiting his friend Rudra's call.

=()=

Imarti

In the small hilly town of Ranikhet lived Mrs. Indira
Sinha. She was a retired school teacher and these days
her only concern was to bring back her husband. Well, Mr.
Romil Sinha was a retired school Principal and he suffered
from Alzheimer's; it was almost an year back that by sheer
mistake Mrs. Sinha forgot to lock her main door and her
husband walked away never to come back. But she was not
among the people who gave up on anything so easily, she was
determined that one day she would bring him back.

My name is Sarla and my family lives in the same colony
as Mrs. Sinha. Our colony is small and it consists of only 10
houses. Our society was a little way up on the mountains,
slightly secluded from the hustle bustle of the town below.
We were surrounded by those huge mountains on the sides
and at the back we had a sort of a forest area. It was a
beautiful place to live. Our homes were not huge but the view
we had of the valley below and of the mountains high up
above us, it was really priceless. Ours was a small knit group
and that is the reason Mr. Sinha's sudden disappearance left

everyone in despair. We all tried for months to find him. We all even reported it to the local police; they tried their best to find him but then all in vain.

Amma, my mother she used to tell Indu aunty to have faith in god that one day he will bring back her husband. But the most surprising thing was that somewhere we all were concerned for Mr. Sinha's disappearance but Indu Aunty was confident that he would comeback. It was as if she secretly knew where he was. Her whole attitude towards the situation was a little surprising for all of us. Somewhere we all were expecting her to throw herself in the throes of despair, maybe cry all day long; but no that was something which she never did. On the contrary she everyday used to make a sweet called Imarti. It kind of became a ritual. Every evening at four she used to leave her house with a bowl full of her delicious smelling Imartis and when she used to return it always used to be empty.

Everyone in our society was a little flummoxed with her behaviour but then no one was that nosy to go and ask her the secret behind cooking Imartis daily. They all discarded it with the thought that maybe she has lost it because she was so much in love with her husband and his sudden disappearance has left her emotionally stranded and thus this strange behaviour. But I on the other hand was very curious about what conspired with the Imartis; so one day when she left at four with the bowl full of Imartis I followed her cautiously, so that she wouldn't notice me following her.

From our society gate she took a left which used to go to our small market area. The walk was a little tricky as it was a steep slope going down the hill. There were huge Deodar trees around us on the hills on the right side and the other side presented a beautiful picture of our town. On a normal day I would really have loved this serene nature walk but today I was all charged up and I was desperate to know the reason where she took those Imartis or what she did with them.

The long walk into the market ended and we now entered the crowded little market. She kept on walking till she reached a point where the homeless people used to sit outside the Shiv temple. She greeted them with a beautiful smile and they reciprocated her in the same way. It was as if she knew them because the camaraderie between her and them was very palpable. I hid myself behind a tea stall from where I had a view of the whole bizarre scenario in front of me. I thought maybe she would go inside the temple and offer the sweets to get her husband back; but she didn't go inside the temple. Instead she started serving the homeless people the Imartis. After that she went inside the temple and came back after a while all smiling and happy. She waved them while going back and then she started again for her home. For a moment the whole situation left me a little perplexed, I didn't get her. It was just before that I was about to go that the tea stall owner an old man said "She comes here every day and gives everyone Imartis. Alternate days she gives Imartis to all of us her in the market and you know what she says to us? Well, she says that I am giving you two, one is for you and the other for a man who is my husband and he is lost. And then she shows us the picture of him and says that if we stumble upon him that day anywhere we should give him this Imarti. So strange it is." Well, as if I was not confused that this tete-a-tete with him confused me even more.

I decided that I would go and ask Indu Aunty what was the secret behind giving everyone an Imarti. But before I could go and confront her she came back and stood in front of me. She said "Sarla, I was a teacher and we are gifted observers. I knew you have been following me since a long time and you even saw me distribute Imartis. I know you have a lot of questions going on in your mind, well let's sit in a cafe nearby as I am tired with the walk and I could really use some good coffee."

It was not yet the tourist season and so we could find a place easily in one of the best cafe in town. We took a window seat as Indu Aunty said that it gave beautiful view of the yonder hills. We ordered coffee and some sandwiches to munch; she took off her glasses and looked at me and said "Well, Sarla I got married in 1965. My family was a very conventional orthodox family. You know I completed my education after I got married. Anyway, Romil came to see me one summer evening. Everyone was excited in the family as I was the first one to get married. But my grandmother had laid down a few ground rules and one of them was that Romil would not get to see me until he said yes. Well we all objected to this but then you know her say was always the last in family and so your Uncle never saw me till our first night. I was kind of a blind date for him or maybe a risk he took. So you must be a little confused as to how he could have said yes to spend the rest of his life with someone whom he didn't even get to see. The answer is simple, he was a complete foodie and I was a good cook. That day my grandmother made me cook Imarti especially for him, as she firmly believed in the saying that way to a man's heart is through his stomach. That really worked, he absolutely loved my Imartis and without even seeing me he said that he would marry me. So we got married all thanks to my Imarti and you know beta for the last 50 years that we have been married he has been madly in love with Imartis." She paused to take a sip from the coffee that just arrived piping hot and then she said again "After he left that day, I decided that I will give two Imartis to everyone in the market area; be it a homeless person or a businessman or a vendor or anyone for that matter. And I always show them his picture and ask them to give one Imarti out of two to this man if they ever see him. I am so certain beta that one day after eating my Imarti he will remember me and come back home. Maybe you can say that is a crazy idea but this is my only hope to bring him back."

We left the coffee shop after awhile and silently we made our way to the society. I was thinking how beautiful her gesture is to get her husband back and I really prayed to god that day to please make her wish come true.

Epilogue- It was four months after that finally one day a fruit vendor who used to come from hills up above us came with Mr. Sinha. He said that as she has told him, he gave one Imarti to this man whom he found resting under the tree in shabby clothes; he said he could make out from the picture that she showed him that this has to be the man from the picture. The fruit vendor said the moment he took the first bite he said no one in this world but his Indu could make Imartis like this and then he started sobbing. The fruit vendor said he then brought him here. He too had tears in his eyes when he saw them both hugging each other as if they would never let the other go.

Indu aunty and Romil Uncle are now back together all thanks to her Imartis.

=()=

Grandpa Mani

Part I

I took a taxi from Chatrapati Shivaji International airport for Dadar West. I am coming back to the city after an interval of 15 long years. I sat straight in the speeding taxi and watched the buildings go by. Mumbai has changed a lot; what it was when I left, and now what it is - there's a huge difference. But I guess there is one thing in Mumbai that would never change -its undeniable spirit; a spirit that lets you dream, and makes you work hard for it no matter what! Long back here, even I dreamed of going to the America for higher education and at that time my dream was unreal to me, but thanks to Grandpa Mani that it came true. Today I have returned to the city after these long years just to meet him. I have a little guilt conscious too, because I didn't keep in touch with him over the years, and he must have felt bad. But knowing Grandpa Mani well, he must have discarded my behaviour with a casual smile as was his wont. He was generous and forgiving at heart, always. That was my Grandpa Mani.

I slowly closed my eyes, and travelled back in time, when I was a boy of 7 and full of dreams about my future life. We lived in a chawl in Dadar west; it was an old building, I guess almost 90 years old, with apartments on all four sides and a big courtyard in the middle, which was used for a lot of things but mainly for us children to play. Baba, my father, used to say that we are lucky that we have a moderately spacious living space, and such a big area to play, which was a blessing in Mumbai. Our family only comprised of three members - Baba, Ma and me. But, No. I guess it would be unfair on my part if I wouldn't include Grandpa Mani. He was a family member for everyone here in our chawl. I guess there was no one who didn't like Grandpa Mani. It was hard not to like him.

Well, let me say more about Grandpa Mani. He is a retired army officer; he took retirement after the war of 65. His full name is Manilal Dhansukhlal Shah. But, fondly we all used to call him Grandpa Mani. Actually, it was Grandpa Mani who suggested that we call him that, and somehow we all loved it. So, it got attached to him and he was known in the whole area as Grandpa Mani. He was a jovial person, always laughing and making people laugh. He was gregarious and always happy to be around. Grandpa Mani also knew many stories and that was one reason he was so famous among the kids. I still recall, every day at sharp 9 after dinner, all children used to flock to Grandpa Mani's place for his famous story time. By just stories he used to take us to different countries, those faraway places that we never even heard of. Every night, there used to be some exciting story, and we all used to love the story time with him, because, maybe in just stories, at least we would travel around the world and that was fun for all of us. He used to take us to a magical land full of adventures with his super power of words. Everyone had some special story by Grandpa Mani which was their favourite, but my favourite was "Escapades of Binni –in America"; well he had this unique way of storytelling in which he used to make every person a hero in his stories, and for me my own heroic tale was my favourite. My name is Binoy and he used to call me Binni. I guess, somehow this name got attached to me, and even now people refer to me as Binni; all thanks to Grandpa Mani.

Grandpa Mani's wife died when I was one, and so I never saw her, and nor did my friends. He used to live all by himself. Sometimes he used to go to Gujarat because he had some farming land there, and to look after that he used to be away from us, which would be an agonizing time for all of us. Grandpa Mani always said that after we all grow up, he will go back to his village and will do farming, and he really was fond of that. He liked everyone, but somehow he had a soft corner for me. I also knew that Grandpa Mani was a little partial towards me, and that's the reason I sometimes used to ask him for things my parents refused to get for me. He was my Santa Claus.

Years passed by quickly, we all friends were done with our graduations and somewhere everyone was figuring out what should be their next step. But, I was certain what my next step would be - going to America for my masters. But, Baba refused as he didn't have that kind of money. He also had to think about his old age. Baba was a senior clerk at an office and so was my Mother, so our budget was a little tight string. By Baba's statement I was thrown in the dumps of despair as that was the only thing I have dreamed of as child, and now I was at wits end as to how to go on about my life if my sole dream is snatched away. To me it felt as if someone has just murdered my dream, and I was left gasping for some ray of hope again in my life; maybe something to cling on to.

It was during that time that Grandpa Mani came to my rescue. He never told me or anyone how he got that amount of money, but he did, and somehow he also convinced my parents to take it in fulfilling my dreams. I remember, as he was talking to my Baba, I was eavesdropping from the other room; he was saying "Arnab, I have no one to call family but you all here in this chawl. You all are my family. And, you all know I have also been very fond of Binni, so when the time has come that I can really help him realize his dream, then why not..? He is like a son or a grandson I never had and never will; so why not allow me to help him in his dream. Binni really wants it Arnab, do not kill his dream. And don't worry about me, I have enough to carry me through hundred years to come. Plus, in helping my Binni, I have a secret dream of mine too. You know, I have always wanted to go to America and visit New York. I have so far seen it only in movies and read about it in books. But, I really want to go there, visit the Metropolitan museum of art, then go to statue of liberty, then taking a picture at Times square, and lastly visiting Harlem. I am sure after Binni finishes his college; he'll land up a good job there and will take his Grandpa Mani at least once to New York. So you see it's basically my dream and Binni is just helping. So stop saying no Arnab and let the boy live his dream." Baba and Ma couldn't say no to Grandpa Mani. I came to America, not just to live my own dream, but Grandpa Mani's too.

Part II

The taxi screeched to halt before the chawl in Dadar where I grew up. I got down, took my luggage and paid the driver. I stood there looking at the structure which was a little dilapidated now, so many memories came rushing back; there's so much that this place has given me and somehow in my life there in America I forgot all about it. Ten years back, even Baba and Ma came to America to stay with us, and then the tie was broken with this city, this place forever. A tear rolled down my cheek, how I could be so mean that I forgot all about Grandpa Mani over these years. All these years, Baba kept telling me that I should write to him and invite him over; but I in my rush to make money, forgot all about that man who helped me in realizing my dream. I was so mean that I forgot all about his dream. The life that I was so proud about was something that I owed to Grandpa Mani. I somehow managed to gather myself, and walked towards the big wrought iron gate, which now was kind of hanging loose; once was an impressive one, now was just a weak reminder of the past.

Grandpa Mani's quarters were on the ground level; I walked up to his door and stood there remembering how many times as a kid I have ran past this wooden door which was always open for candies, for help in history lessons, for story time and sometimes just to talk my heart out. Grandpa Mani's image just flashed across my eyes; he was tall, a bit frail maybe because of his age, his big blue eyes and those big curly moustaches. Well, he was a man no one could ever hate; it was only love that you would feel for him. The kindness in his voice and those gentle big blue eyes only demanded love. I knocked on the door and took a few step backwards, waiting for that man who made me fulfil my dream to open the door with his quintessential ear to ear grin. After what felt like an eternity to me, I heard the squeak of his wheel chair, and the door flew open, and there he was smiling at me with those big blue eyes and that smile, which was a little weak now. He rolled out his chair towards me and asked me to give him a hug; he said it's been ages Binni, where have you been? He said, "Look I got old waiting for you", and gave me a friendly punch on the shoulders.

I collapsed on my knees, and put my head on his lap and cried. I must have been crying for a long time, Grandpa Mani kept stroking my hair gently, and then finally he said that I'll drench him and he is not even wearing his raincoat. I smiled at him; he always had the knack making any moment lighter with his funny remarks. I went inside his apartment and it was just the same as I had remembered. The same old cane furniture and those two big wooden closets, his big canopy wooden bed and his wheelchair and pictures of his wife everywhere. Well, Grandpa Mani had to retire because he was injured in the war of 65; he lost his legs in the war. But, that loss never ever dampened his spirits.

I was sitting there on the cane chair when Grandpa Mani ordered the little boys playing outside to get some tea and vada-pavs. He then came and sat beside me in his wheelchair. I had a lot to say to him, but somehow I couldn't muster up the courage to tell him. After a long silence between us, I asked Grandpa Mani to forgive me;

I said "I do not know when and how I forgot about you. I shouldn't have, Grandpa. You were the one who helped me realize my dream, and that too by selling your land in your village. Now, don't look at me that way with disbelief, I know you got that money by selling your land. Why did you do that for me..? I went there, and then somehow just got so involved in other things that I completely forgot that you were waiting for me here, and that it's my turn now to help you in realizing your dream. I feel rotten, Grandpa Mani. I mean, I was not like this. But, I don't know how I forgot all about you, until my little daughter Swara once browsing through my old pictures saw our picture together at the garden and asked all about you. It was then for first time that I told my kids about you, and then it all came rushing back to me. I was a rotten person, Grandpa. How could I forget all about you when it was because of you that I was there? It's not late Grandpa now, please come with me to America. I have come here to take you with me. Please do not say no. I want you there; I want you to live your dream now. I have lived mine, it's your turn now. I am sorry, but I promise I'll make up for all the years that I forgot about you. Please Grandpa Mani, come with me. My wife, my kids they all are eager to meet you. I have told them everything about you and they are just dying to see you, to be with you. Please forgive me. Give me one more chance."

For some moments he didn't say anything at all. He just kept looking at me, and then he beckoned me come near him; and he pulled my ear, I was totally surprised when he did this. He always used to gently pull my ears whenever I used to do something bad, it was his way for reprimanding me. He then hugged me and I knew that he has forgiven me. Well, Grandpa Mani was like that, he could never stay angry with anyone ever for long. He always used to say that life is very short, so instead of holding grudges, let's forgive people and give love another chance. I was very happy that he gave me another chance. I was rotten with him, but he still was the same person. Over the years, his love for me never changed; even when I didn't turn up for fifteen long years. Well, that's my Grandpa Mani. The most wonderful person you will ever meet.

Epilogue- Today we went to see the statue of liberty and the expression of joy I saw on his face was priceless. I love Grandpa Mani and now will never ever let him go away from me. I needed him back then, and I need him now. I want my children to have the same wonderful memories that I have, as kid, with Grandpa Mani.

8:50 Ki Fast Local

Part I

Mumbai is a city of dreams. People flock to this city with
hearts full of dreams and aspirations for a good life. This city
has always welcomed people with open arms and it continues
to do so. Well, this story is about seven women who used to
travel from the suburb of Borivali to their respective offices
and college in Churchgate. Let's take a peek into their lives
that they so loved and let's travel with them on the 8:50's
fast local to Churchgate.

It's already 8:15 and Sumitra is yet to get out of her
home; it's one of those days for her when her mother-in-law
gets gripped by her severe arthritis and she could not help
Sumitra pack lunch for Abhay, Sumitra's husband and for her
only daughter Radhika. Sumitra is always so grateful for her
Ma-in-law's help and she never ever ceases the opportunity
to thank her. She is literally a blessing to Sumitra and she
is the sole reason that Sumitra has been able to continue her
job even after getting married. Sumitra and Abhay had an
arranged marriage and they have a rock solid relationship

for the past 18 years now. They had Radhika after 3 years of being married and she was their angel in disguise and they both just dote on their daughter and are very proud about the fact that she is doing so well academically. They try their best to give her everything possible but being a middle-class Mumbaikar is a little tough but their daughter understands fully. She has never complained about their one-bedroom-hall-kitchen apartment; or the fact that her parents do not have a car. She has been a good daughter for them. Sumitra's mother-in-law is a retired school teacher and gets a modest pension, and she tries to help in every way possible. Her father-in-law passed away two years back and they all still miss him. Life is tough but with love and hard work they manage it beautifully.

Ritu as usual has arrived way before time of the train, as she loves observing people in their daily mundane routine. Ritu is the only daughter of the bank officials Mr. And Mrs. Roy. Both her parents have a bank job with a nationalized bank and have been working with the bank for years. They have a fairly good accommodation in Borivali and absolutely love the city. They came to Mumbai almost 31 years ago; they were young and just married and had landed this bank job and were super excited for their new life in Mumbai. Ritu was born to them after 4 years of being married and they just doted on their daughter and fussed about her a lot and that they still do. Ritu's mother despite her protests packs her lunch and makes such a fuss about her going to the office and that sometimes it irks her but deep down she just loves her parents a lot and knows that she's their world and they are hers. She is 27 and has a good job with a fashion house and she simply loves her job and is a dedicated worker.

For Damini life has changed totally after her bitter divorce two years back. She loved her husband too much and it took her a long time to understand and grasp the fact that he has been cheating on her for like a long time, while she was busting her ass working and managing the home along with the demanding in-laws and a nagging elder sister-in-law. Back then life has been a constant struggle for her; it's not easy juggling between the roles that she played, of being a wife, a mother, a daughter-in-law and a working woman. It was pretty tough and with zero support from her in-laws and her husband. Ratan has never been supportive of her and her work but she was always determined to work and in the end it proved good for her, as now she can sustain at-least in an economical way with her children and live a life of peace. Ratan agreed in the court to provide her with a particular sum of money every month to help her raise the children and pay for their education. She now lives in cramped one-bedroom-hall and kitchen apartment in Borivali (east), but she is fine with the cramped apartment compared to her earlier cramped life. Damini has two children, both boys and they are 10 and 12 years of age and have been very supportive of their mother through the entire process of the divorce and both of them are well behaved boys. Her life is tough being a single mother but she knows she will cope -up with it.

Sayali loves to get dressed despite the protests from her Aai, that one does not go to college to flaunt oneself but they go to study rather. But Sayali is young and extremely beautiful girl and she loves to get dressed. Her Baba, Mr. Kulkarni has been working with a private company for like years and has a decent income and so does her elder brother

Anirudh and his wife Piyali. They both are working with a private bank and doing really well in their fields. They have a son named Shiv and he is the apple of the eye of everyone in the family and they all just dote on him and spoil him silly. Sayali is a bright girl and made her parents really proud when she got accepted by a very prestigious college in the city. She will be completing her first year of Masters and after the completion of the masters, she plans to do MBA and land a lucrative job. It's been her dream and now she feels that she is really close to making it come true. Sayali lives with her parents and her brother, his wife and Shiv and they all share a two-bedroom apartment in Shimpoli.

Zarana ben Shah and that is how she loves to get spoken about or be referred to. She is a simple and sweet Guajarati woman who just loves her family a lot and to make the ends meet has been working for the good 15 years of her married life and with no complaints. Her family has been the residents of Mumbai ever since the Brits left the country, and they have a modest accommodation in a chawl in Kalbadevi area of the city. The transition for Zarana ben was pretty easy after getting married; as she used to live in a cramped one room and kitchen chawl space with a family that consisted 7 members. After marriage she moved to the Suburb of Borivali with her husband and has been living in the same apartment for the past 15 years. Life has been good to Zarana ben, as her husband loves her immensely and her in-laws are very fond of her, though they don't live in the city but still whenever they come, they are all praise about her and she absolutely loves that. It's just one thing that is missing from their hunky-dory picture and that is the fact that they are childless. It's been 15 years since they have trying to conceive but in vain. But still her faith is so strong that she still believes that even after 15 years of being childless, one day she will have a baby and even her home would be aloud with the little feet and their chirpy voices. Today she is really happy as it's her husband's birthday and she is planning a surprise party for him and has even taken half-day leave from the office. She just couldn't wait to tell all her train friends about her plans.

Prajakta is really tensed today, as she has to compeer a program today at the college and despite the encouragement and good words from her colleagues she is at wits end and really nervous. She is a beautiful woman in her late thirties and works as a professor with a prestigious college in town. She has a daughter and a son and both her kids are a menace at home and sometimes get totally out of hand but still are good kids with zest for learning. Prajakta lost her husband in the terror attack of 2008. Prashant was working at a really good position with a multinational and was at the Taj with some clients when this unfortunate thing happened. Her world came crumbling down right in front of her own eyes. Even now she cannot believe the fact that Prashant is dead. They were together in the college and it was love at first sight for them. They both were madly in love and were inseparable till his end. He came from a Punjabi family and she came from a strict Maharashtrian Brahmin family but this never came between them, as they beautifully blended both the worlds. They got married right after college, as they both landed great jobs and were eager to start their new life. They would have celebrated their 10th wedding anniversary if that incident wouldn't have happened. Now she is all by herself and her children are the only remembrance she has of him. Her parents and in-laws live in the same city and even offered her to come and move with them but she declined, she wants to be in this apartment which she and Prashant so lovingly bought and decorated. She cannot do this to his memory. Prashant lives in her heart and for her he'll always be the only man.

Tanya Mascarenas is a beautiful and petite woman in her forties and has been a working woman ever since she was 21. She was an out and out Mumbaikar and loved the city for its pace and its spirit. Her husband Peter owned a small restaurant in the suburb of Borivali where they lived and they used to cater authentic Goan cuisine; it was doing fairly good and with her added income they could live comfortably. She had three children; two girls and one boy. Her son Savio was the oldest one and just recently he landed a job with a prestigious company in the US and that made him the first Mascarenas to go abroad. Everyone in the entire clan, including the extended family was super happy and very proud of Savvy, as he was dearly called. He was just 24 and according to Tanya very young to go abroad all by him. She wanted to get him married but he was adamant and kept refusing. Finally she had to give up on him and with half-heart she started his packing for US. Her two daughters, Alice and Tina were in college and they too like their elder brother were studying Engineering. Tanya's in-laws also lived with her and they were a big jolly and happy group which lived in the I.C colony area of Borivali in a three-bedroom kitchen apartment, which was bought by Peter's father some 42 years back. Today Tanya was very happy because she was going to meet her train friends after a gap of four days and she was in super mood and had even baked her famous chocolate and cherry cake for everyone, and it was eggless because Zarana ben was a strict vegetarian.

Harleen Kaur was big burly woman and at the first glance she gave an impression of being a woman wrestler but she was apparently not and was working at the most renowned Museum in Mumbai. She had deep knowledge and respect for the art and its connoisseurs. She hailed from New Delhi and had been a resident of Mumbai for the past 18 years but still she missed Delhi and especially the food. She was married to Amrinder Singh Ahluwalia who was by profession a dentist but just like his wife he too gave the impression of being a member of the Indian wrestling team. Dr. Ahluwalia was good in his work and has earned a good reputation in the suburb of Borivali. They were blessed with a beautiful girl and they named her Simran. She was a beautiful girl and the total opposite of her parents, as she was petite and tiny. She was in her 12th grade and she aspired to be an army officer one day.

It was almost 8.45 and everyone was now at the station waiting for the train. Train arrived promptly and they all rushed into the ladies compartment and sat at their usual place. Zarana Ben was seemed very happy today and everyone said that she was even looking special today; they it was her hubby's birthday. Tanya opened her Tupperware box and she gave a piece of cake to everyone. Tanya was all talk about Savvy; they told her he would be all fine, as he is a grown up person now. But who can argue with a worried mother. Sayali was reprimanding Tanya for spoiling her with this cake, as she was on a weight watch program. But then no one she thought could say no to Tanya's Choco cherry cake, it's simply out of this world. Damini and Sumitra were in a deep discussion about how to marinate paneer for tikkas; Sayali was too busy eating her share of cake and feeling guilty about it at the same time. Tanya, Harleen and Zarana ben every busy discussing the weather, but Prajakta was tensed too tensed today. It was after they crossed Andheri that everyone realized that Prajakta was not talking at all, she was just staring out of the window. It was Sayali who asked her the matter, and she said that the compeering was worrying her. But this baffled everyone; Prajakta has been in this field for almost thirteen years now, so why all of a sudden this kind of fear and nervousness. Tanya sensed that there was more to it and she was not telling everyone the full story. But then they didn't force her, as they knew that by evening Prajakta would spill the beans. They all got up as Churchgate was next station. They got down at the station, said goodbyes and dispersed to their respective places.

It was around 6.30 in the evening that everyone gathered again at the Churchgate station. Prajakta was the last to arrive and she was not alone, she walked into the station with a dashing looking man; he must have been in his late 30's. He was very tall, he wore black framed spectacles and he carried with himself a sleek leather case. Prajakta and that man were talking animatedly and somehow they didn't realize that the rest of the group was watching them very intently. It was when the train arrived, that Prajakta and that guy spilt up, she walked into the ladies compartment with everyone and he got into the general one.

After they crossed Dadar that they got their regular seats; once settled Sumitra and Tanya both pounced on Prajakta as to who was she talking to so intently. Prajakta just brushed aside saying, "Oh that guy well his name is

Ayush and he too is a professor with me. Earlier he was working for a MNC but then he realized that his calling was teaching, so he gave up his lucrative job in the multinational and joined our college. You girls, do not run your imaginary horses, okay..?"

Ten days passed and it kind of became a ritual that Prajakta would walk in to the station with Ayush and then they would disperse after the train arrived. It was one such evening while returning home that Zarana Ben said to Prajakta, "Prajakta I do not have any right what so ever to interfere in your personal life but trust me this Ayush guy thinks of you more than a friend. I mean there's something called friendship and something called love; and what I see for you in his eyes, actually not just me but we all firmly think that he loves you and somewhere you are stopping him from coming close to you. I understand totally that you still feel married to Prashant, but Prajakta on a serious note you are young and how long you think you would go on living life like that. I mean like a saint. You deserve happiness and companionship once again. Do not shy away from it dear. Give life another chance." Even Sayali and Ritu chirped in saying, "Prajakta see if you do not do anything about this guy then mind you we will snatch him away from you. I mean God!! He is so good looking and the way he looks at you makes our heart melt away yaar. Common don't be so stingy, give him a chance." Damini and Harleen somewhere understood the spot Prajakta was in, well especially Damini understood. She was living alone with her children and she too craved for some companionship; she said sometimes she used to dream of getting married for the second time and this time to the right person, maybe her Mr. Right. Damini told her to at least give it a try maybe not just for her but for her kids too. Harleen and Prajakta were close, so Harleen told her that there is nothing wrong with falling in love for the second time; she said in no way you would be disrespecting Prashant's memory. Harleen said Prajakta women are strong creatures and they can live without a man and its nothing wrong but she said I have seen admiration and liking for Ayush in your eyes and if you won't do anything about it then you would defying your own feelings. Don't do that.

It took everyone a lot of effort to convince Prajakta to at least go out with him once or twice and see how it goes. Tanya said, "Look darling we are not pushing you to the altar but dating is no crime and what if you fall in love. So try it baby. I have my old man at home you see otherwise you never stood a chance with Ayush. Just kidding dear; go for coffee and see how things go, at least you'll get to know him outside college and Churchgate station."

Well it took all their persuasion power for two months that finally Prajakta said yes to Ayush's proposal for a coffee. It was decided that they would meet up for coffee on Saturday in Bandra. Ritu and Sayali made a lot of fuss about what Prajakta should wear and what kind of makeup she should put on; Prajakta was so overwhelmed with all this that at one point she was in total mood to call up Ayush and cancel the date but it was Zarana Ben and Sumitra who stopped her from taking this drastic step.

They all came with her to the station somewhere to make sure she boarded the train and also to support her and tell her silently that they were with her no matter what. Prajakta got on the train to Bandra, and luckily she got a seat near the window. Prajakta's thoughts were going back to all her friends and how they have supported her always. She so remembered that when Prashant passed away, besides her family all her train friends used to drop by at any pretext to her house just to check how she was doing. They all were with her in her moments of agonizing pain and now here she was almost on the brink of a start of a new relationship, and as always they were here for her again. They were the best thing that happened to her of course after Prashant, her parents and her kids.

Part II

It was at 9.05 when the train halted at Andheri station that Ritu almost toppled over another woman in her attempt to see if Prajakta was boarding the train or not. Prajakta was re-joining her college after a break of almost fifteen days. For this special occasion Zarana Ben had prepared besan ladoo and Tanya made Prajakta's favourite brownie muffin. Ritu and Sayali were dying to see the pictures of their honeymoon, well of course the censored ones. It was Damini who saw Prajakta first, she was beaming with happiness and for some reason she was looking even prettier than usual. Prajakta joined in after an initial struggle of making her way past the women who were going to get down on the next station. She almost bumped into Harleen but thankfully Harleen's big burly self protected them both from a fatal fall.

They were all ears to Prajakta's tales of how her honeymoon went. She said she was totally caught by surprise when Ayush told her that instead of honeymooning in Darjeeling they were going to Egypt, which was Prajakta's favourite place and she mentioned to him numerous times when they used to meet up for those casual coffee dates.

Prajakta said that she was never really sure that these casual dates after a year would end up in their marriage. Sumitra told her that they were sure about it though somewhere Prajakta had doubts.

They all got down at Churchgate station and were starting to go off to their respective work places, when Harleen shouted out to everyone and she literally embraced everyone in her big bear hug. She said she was so happy today that she wanted to start her day with getting a cosy big hug from her most beloved people.

Epilogue- They all still travel to their work every day and their lives are going on. There are a few changes though now. Sayali has gotten engaged to a guy she has been dating for a while; Ritu has changed her job, she has moved to a bigger fashion house in Bandra. Zarana Ben is still hoping that someday her house would be aloud with tiny feet. Sumitra is happy in her own sweet world, and her daughter is fairing really well in academics. Tanya is happy as her Savio is all set in the states now. Damini is at peace with her life and hopes someday she too just like Prajakta would find a soul mate; well it's not that she is unhappy right now but it would be amazing if she had someone to rely on or share her worries and fear with. Prajakta is super happy with Ayush and even her kids are very happy with him; though it took some time for them to accept him but now they are inseparable.

=()=

Manicure For Ma

Part I

Kavya's tiny frame was slouched against the grimy window of the bus, and her deep set brown eyes were gazing past the traffic and chaos she was passing through. Her blue and yellow salwar-kameez was all crumpled, but that was the last thing on her mind today. All she could think at the moment was her home, and especially the surprise she has planned for her Ma's birthday. Kavya was nervous and excited at the same time about the surprise she had planned for her mother; before coming to the conclusion she went through a lot of things in her mind, but nothing could ever come close to this one. She was just waiting to see the look on her mother's face, these minutes seemed like ages to Kavya.

Finally for Kavya those agonizing moments came to an end when she got down at the crowded bus depot at Byculla. It was raining hard today, the quintessential Mumbai rains but even the rains could not dampen the excitement she was filled with. Kavya took her umbrella and started walking through the crowd; this bus depot was like home to her and so it was easy for her to make her way in this rain and with people crowding all over. Her parents used to live in a chawl here in Byculla and it's been there home for almost 28 years now. Kavya has grown up here, and no matter what the condition of the place, to her it still was home and even those outer walls with the hideous posters of b-grade movies, the tattered paint, and those things never bothered her because it was her home, a place where she belonged.

Kavya made her way quickly to the staircase that led to her first floor room and on her way, even though she was a little late she could not forget to blow a kiss to 'Azoba' (as one calls grandfather in Marathi), who lived next door, and ever since she could remember he's been the same. There were too many memories associated with him, and he was an integral part of Kavya's life, what she was and now is.

The old rusted door handle was still the same, and even the picture of Lord Ganesha was still there. She could hear her mother getting up from that squeaky chair, which she so loved. Her mother opened the door with her quintessential smile; Kavya hugged her tightly and wished her a wonderful birthday. Her mother was a little embarrassed about the whole birthday affair that her family has been planning for her. In her life of 60 years she has never ever celebrated her birthday and so all this fuss about her birthday was kind of overwhelming to her; but she was happy too at the same time, because all her family was together and there was nothing in the world for her which came closer to family. She doted on them and showered all her love on them. Her little room was full with people who were her world; her husband of 40 years Girdhari, her two sons, their wives, her grandchildren, her two daughters.

The moment Kavya had wished her mother her elder sister and her two sister-in-laws grabbed her by the arm and took her to a secluded corner they could find in the little room. They were her co-conspirators in planning the gift for her mother and they all were nervous and excited at the same time about it.

Part II

Kavya and her siblings were born to Girdhari and Mala who were struggling to find their footing in India's biggest metropolis. They were originally from Latur, and they, like many others, came to Mumbai with dreams of making it big someday and for which they were ready to work hard. Girdhari started work at a factory and retired as foreman. Mala too had to work, as her husband's salary was not sufficient for them to survive with four children. She was not much educated and the only work that she could find was as a maid. She was efficient and all her employers relied on her a lot. It's been a long time that she has ceased to work because now there was no need.

All these years that Mala had worked for the rich and elite of Mumbai, she has always been fascinated by one thing, and that was all the women she used to work for had immaculate and lovely manicured hands painted with beautiful nail colors. She, on the other hand used to look at her own hard and calloused hands, and used to wonder that will she ever be able to have hands like them, even for a day. But wishes are like horses and this wish for her sadly never came true.

On her 60th Birthday Kavya, her sister and her sisters-in-law had planned a visit for Mala at one of the best Salons in the city and they knew that she is going to object to it, because she would surely realize that they have spent a lot on it. But, deep down they all knew that she was going to love it and it was going to be the best gift for her.

After cutting the cake and taking her husband's blessing, Kavya took her mother by the arm and told her to keep quiet and just go with the flow. Mala was a bit surprised and as she was instructed she kept quiet all the way to the Salon. It was one of the best Salons in Mumbai, and Mala was a bit shocked and surprised to be there.

Kavya went and spoke to the girl on the reception desk and confirmed her appointment. They had to wait for some time and then her mother was escorted to the area where the manicures and pedicures were done. For Mala, this was all new and totally foreign and she felt really uncomfortable in her simple Cotton sari with a small zari border. All the women around her were either wearing westerns, or even those who were wearing Indian clothes were definitely wearing designer ones according to Mala. But the moment her manicure started her attention was drawn completely to what the girl would do to make her calloused hands beautiful.

Kavya was watching her mother in delight and she knew this was worth it. After her mother's manicure was completed with a nail color of her choice applied on her now beautiful hands, Kavya just couldn't help noticing that beautiful smile on her mother's face. That smile spoke a lot which words could defy and Kavya knew this gift was worth a million dollars.

Kavya and her mother walked out of the Salon and her mother couldn't keep her eyes off her hands. They looked beautiful and she had tears of joy in her eyes. She was beaming with happiness and she was at loss of words to thank her children. This was the best gift of her life and she knew that she will cherish it forever.

6 O'clock At Five Gardens

Part I

Rajaram Deshmukh left his residential quarters at exact 5:45 in the evening as was his wont. He and his friends used to meet every evening at the five gardens and it was a ritual no one ever missed. Rajaram used to walk his way to the park as he lived nearby and also he was very fond of walking. He was an out and out Mumbaikar and he always used to say that walking was in his genes. Rajaram was 76 years old and it's been almost 16 years since he retired from his LIC job. He had two children, both boys and by god's grace they were always brilliant in studies and they made their way to the IIT's on their own; it was their sheer hard work and perseverance that they shone brightly at the IIT's and during their final year both of them landed jobs at really good companies and after a few years they shifted to the states for good. He had twins and today it was their birthday both of his children turned 48. Rajaram was also blessed with four grand children and now two of them were in the college too. Rajaram lived in Mumbai with his wife of 50 years, Asavari. They had a small one-bedroom-hall and kitchen apartment in Dadar. It was a small space but the couple was in love with their home and they cherished it completely.

Just when he was entering the park, Rajaram heard someone shout his name and even before he turned he knew it was Mangya (Mangesh, he was fondly called Mangya). Mangya also lived nearby and their evening meetings were sacred to him and he and no one ever missed it. Both Rajaram and Mangya entered the park and went to their usual place near the tree at the corner of the park and they eagerly waited for the others to come. This evening meeting has been their ritual for the past 40 years and they all looked forward to it.

The group comprised of six members, they were a potpourri of different cultures and beliefs all mingled into one. There was Rajaram, then Mangya, Rustom Daruwala, Subba Ayengar, Robert Fonseca, Gora Bannerjee. They all were almost the same age and were retired now. Rustom lived nearest to the garden at the "Dadar parsi colony", his family has been living there since 90 years. He was a retired bank cashier and he shared his apartment with his wife Fanny and his son Boman and his 97 year old mother. Subba too lived in Dadar and has been a resident of Mumbai ever since 45 years; he came to Mumbai from Pudducherry when he was transferred. He too retired as a bank cashier at the same bank where Rustom used to work. Subba and his wife lived all alone, as they were childless. Rajaram and Mangya both were working at the LIC and were friends since a long time. Mangya and his wife lived with their daughter Sayali; Sayali was a school teacher and was

a widow and she had one son Shekhar, who was in his final
year of Engineering. Robert and his wife Daisy were born
and brought up in Mumbai and they had two sons and both
their sons were married and had their own family. Their sons
ran a very successful bakery and lived in Bandra with their
family. Gora and his wife Indrani were all alone. They had
one son, but he died in a road accident some 25 years ago
and ever since then they both were all alone. But the void
which his son left was somewhere filled by his dear friends.

It was by 6:15 all the other members also joined in.
Vishnu came with their cup of masala tea and bun. Vishnu
too has been here at the park for long; he had a small lorry
near the garden and he used to sell tea and vada-pavs (the
staple Mumbai food). He came from Kanpur almost 31 years
back with dreams of making himself a good life here in
Mumbai, but unfortunately his dreams never came true and
to sustain himself and his family in this big metropolis he
started selling tea and Vada-pavs and made a decent living
of it. He has been serving tea to this group for 25 years now
and sometimes when he did not have many customers he
also used to join the gang and used to chit –chat with them
and share funny anecdotes with them in his typical Kanpur
accent.

Kabir Kaul is a writer and he aspires to come up with
a writer's house, a concept that will give platform to new
writers like him and will give them assistance in getting
their work published. Kabir came to Mumbai from Jammu
almost ten years back with dreams of making it big in the
literary world but it's been ten years since then and all he
was able to publish was a book of essays. To sustain himself
in this big city he was forced to find another job; he works

at a fashion house in Parel as a fashion blogger. He doesn't like his job but to sustain himself he has to do that. Kabir's office is in Parel and ever since he joined it he used to come to the five gardens around 6:15 and used to sit here with his laptop and he used to write short stories on everyday life; his dream was to get this published but how that he was not aware of. He was a regular at the five gardens here in Dadar and he was always amused by the group of Rajaram and his friends. Kabir was not an eavesdropper but he used to sit just besides the bench where this lively elderly group used to sit and sometimes while there used to be a lull in his stories, he used to listen to their animated talks about everything; they literally spoke about everything under the sun; for example, politics, art, theatre, literature, films, life in Mumbai, the changing India, televisions serials, music and everything except their personal lives. Kabir so well remembers that never ever anyone of them has ever spoken about their private lives. That was astonishing and mysterious to him at the same time. He always use to think, that people have problems and they always share it with their loved ones or their friends; but this group was a happy and a very literate group and they never used to bother each other with family issues or their day to day problems. It didn't mean they did not have them, but it only meant that they meant to make their time here in the evening special and stress free. Kabir once heard Gora say that, life should be dealt on a daily basis; he said there is no point in stressing over something that happened or what might happen in the future. According to him one should live in the present and the rest god will take care off. Kabir could never forget these words and it somewhere helped him come out of his depression and melancholic mood.

It wasn't just Kabir who used to notice things about the group but it was vice e versa. They too were quiet observant about him and today Robert decided that he will go talk to this young man and introduce himself and ask him to join the group. Robert and everyone in the group were very friendly and they were always looking for new people to make friends with. It was Friday and as was the ritual, this week it was his turn to bring some homemade snack. Daisy was really good at cupcakes and so he got dozens of them for his friends. He took two walnut cupcakes out of his brown bag and offered it to Kabir. Kabir was engrossed in writing and he was a little surprised when out of now where a cupcake popped in front of him. He looked up and saw a beaming Robert standing there with a cupcake. "Hey there!! I'm Robert, how are you and what's your name..?". It took a few seconds for Kabir to register that Robert was talking to him. He smiled back and introduced himself and took those delicious looking cupcakes. Robert asked Kabir to come and join him and his friends at their usual corner. Kabir accepted the offer, as this group has always caught his attention and he wanted to know their story, their life and most of all he wanted to be friends with them.

Kabir has been suffering from constant bouts of depression and it was majorly to cope up with it that he started coming to the Five gardens. After Robert's generous invitation to join him and the gang to chit chat, that kind of became a ritual for Kabir every day. It was Rajaram who asked him, "Don't you ever hang out with people your age..?". Kabir said he was little shy, plus somehow he never managed to forge a good friendship with anyone here in Mumbai; he said it's been ten years for him here but still there's no one he would call a close friend.

Part II

It's been a year since Kabir started hanging out regularly with the group. Today he was the first to arrive, even earlier than Rajaram Uncle; and it gave him time to think how he was an year back when he first started talking with the group and now he was a completely different person. It was them that he learned that life is not always about complaining for what you do not have but it's rather all about appreciating what you have. Kabir remembered that once Gora Uncle said, "There are so many things in this world to do that we do not have the time to waste on brooding over what we don' have; rather we should use that time to learn something new every single day, every single minute. One should be happy and content with what you have but Kabir this doesn't imply that I am telling you to forget your dream; I am not saying that. Dream, and always dream big but meanwhile the distance between your present life and the dream should not be made melancholic or mundane but rather be happy about who you are and what you are doing. So when your dream is accomplished you can look back and realize that you were the same happy person you are now; that you didn't waste your time in being sad rather you utilized it in being happy and did constructive work. And lastly I'll say enjoy what you are doing otherwise life will be a terrible dread. Trust me." Kabir smiled remembering that after Gora Uncle finished his rather short speech, Robert Uncle got up and did a dramatic clapping for him and everyone laughed.

Kabir thought even Vishnu the tea stall owner is happy when he knows that his dream has vanished away somewhere but that doesn't ever stop him from smiling or making others smile. He was feeling so blessed that he was friends with such people; it when he was reminiscing the year gone by, that Rustom and Mangya walked up to him and gave him a good jolt. Kabir came back to the present. He said, "Good god, you guys should stop calling yourself old, you literally shook me up." Gradually everyone joined in and even Vishnu came today, as Kabir has told everyone that the coming day he has something special to discuss and he wants everyone present. Subba said please Kabir kill the suspense, he said I couldn't even sleep the night before; everyone punched him on the shoulders in a friendly way, he was always dramatizing things. Rajaram had even given him the nickname of "Drama King". Kabir brought everyone back; they all had a bad habit of drifting away from the topic at hand. Kabir opened up the big brown bag, and took out very carefully the cake he had himself baked. He said that finally his book of stories has been selected by a prestigious publishing house in town and next month they would roll out copies. For a moment it felt that everyone was either frozen or dazed; it was Rustom who gave a big yell, drawing out the attention of nearby walkers and hugged Kabir tightly. Then everyone joined in and Kabir was almost smashed to death. Finally they let go off him and they all blessed him with all the success they said he deserved. Vishnu was so happy that he said that today the tea and vada-pavs would be on him. And then they all pounced on the yummy cake that Kabir has baked. Kabir walked a little back from the group and secretly he thanked god that he is blessed with such loving friends and then he too pushed his way in to have some cake.

The Apology

Rati was sitting in the reception area of the hospital and by every passing minute she was getting restless. Her head was still reeling; the effect that phone call had on her seemed would never cease. She closed her eyes and played that scene in her mind over and over again; it was tormenting every time.

She was at the party of one of her closest friend Bindu and it was a great occasion as Bindu's art work was selected to be portrayed at one of India's most premier art gallery. Everyone was happy for Bindu; her years of perseverance and hard work finally landed her this opportunity that she has been waiting for so long. As like Rati, even Bindu was a late starter in life and she deserved every bit of this success and happiness in life. Rati was talking to Sameer when her cell phone rang; it was an unknown number and for a moment she was reluctant to pick the call but then her curiosity got the better of her. She answered the call and the moment the caller on the other line said "hello", Rati just froze. She went numb mentally and physically; she just did not know what to do; should she answer back or just slam down the phone. Her silence was thought as an approval by the person on the other side and without wasting any time, he pleaded her to come and visit him just once; he told her he has something to say to her and which he would not be able to say on phone and thus he pleaded to her to come and visit him once. Rati was dumbfounded; his icy cold voice was pleading to her, she could not believe that a man like him would ever plead to her. She was tempted to say a bold "NO", but then she thought that for at least the past they had shared, she should at least go and meet him once. She knew well that he has given her ample of reasons not to see him for the rest of their lives; she knew he deserved only hate from her but still a small part in her convinced her that for once she should let the past be past and meet him. She said yes and kept the phone, she had no urge to prolong the conversation.

The nurse came and told her that she can now go in and meet him. Rati followed the nurse down the winding corridors of the hospital in a state of daze. It's been 18 years since she has seen him; 18 years since she left her bruised past and started a new life. The nurse halted at the door and stepped aside and asked her to go in and then she left. For a few seconds Rati stood there and she had this urge to run away from him, from the past, from her memories and everything associated with him. But some supernatural power in her urged her to stay and talk to him once.

Rati opened the glass door and walked in to find a tiny caricature of a man lying on the bed; his eyes were closed and he looked too fragile and weak. She sat besides the bed and mustered up the courage to put her hands on his just to wake him up. Slowly he opened his eyes and a faint smile played on his lips. He was looking ten years more of his age and Rati was literally shocked to see him like this.

There was an awkward silence between them and they both were looking for the right words to start the conversation. Rati finally spoke up and she asked him how he was and what happened that he is in such a condition. It took a lot of effort for him to speak up and finally he told her that he's been suffering from brain cancer and he's in the final stages of the disease. He had to pause to take a breath.

Rati was lost in her thoughts again; she went back in time, when she had just entered the Kapoor household with hopes, dreams and love of a future she would have with her husband Ravish. She was just 22 at the time and her heart was filled with just love and love for the future she would have with her husband. But fate had something else in store for Rati and for which she was not at all prepared for. It was on her wedding night that she came face to face with her husband who was an animal. As all girls even Rati imagined her first night to be a night of tender romance and sharing thoughts about life together and so much more lovey-dovey things; but her confrontation was with an animal, who just bruised and abused her body the whole night and then slept leaving her in pain emotionally as well as physically.

Ravish was not just abusive while lovemaking but he even used to beat her up at the smallest of pretexts and he was also abusive verbally. For the society he was a well respected man, who ran his business impeccably, and was successful at a very young age; but for Rati he was a nightmare from which she so wanted to run. For Rati life was hell and there was no escape too; her parents were too old school and they always used to tell her to bear everything as he was her husband. There was no logic in the argument her parents gave but then she had no option back then and not enough strength to fight for herself; even her in-laws failed to understand her predicament and Rati was left alone in her battle. She also got pregnant after a year of marriage and gave birth to two beautiful boys. They were named Luv and Kush.

Her life was a constant struggle everyday and after a while she became numb to pain. Thankfully for Rati, at least her husband had the decency to limit his abusive behaviour to their bedroom and her boys never came to know what an animal their father was. For Rati her endurance and patience were thinning with years and she was getting tired of explaining to her kids the bruised marks on her body and face.

She still remembered, it was stormy night and her husband was sleeping and she was silently crying in pain after their sexual encounter. It was then that Rati decided that enough is enough and she cannot bear it any longer. She knew full well, she had no place to go but still she was determined to get out of the house. She threw some clothes in a bag and took all her jewellery and some cash; the hardest part was yet to come. She knew that she would not be able to take her children with her because she was yet to find a place to live and a source of income and till then she thought they have to stay here.

She left a note for him and left the house for good, for her own good. She was surprised that she has spent so many years in this house and yet when she left she felt nothing; there was no regret or remorse in her and she knew that Ravish has given her so many wounds emotionally and physically that she would never ever miss this part of her life, rather she just wanted to erase it forever from her memories.

It took a while for Rati to find a footing for herself but she eventually did it and she even fought in the court for the custody of her children and she got that too; finally the table was turning on her side and she could see a tiny ray of hope in her bleak world. Rati was always a gifted writer and her job at a publication gave her the right opportunity to write. She started off by writing for the magazine's agony aunt section and then slowly and gradually she became their one of the most sought after short story writer. It took years for Rati to be where she was, because at age 37 she started her life from scratch with her two children, but then despite her scarred past she did manage to get a good life for herself and her children.

Rati recovered from her trance and she came back to the present. Ravish was looking into oblivion, he was staring in space, like a lost soul. After a while he spoke up again and he told Rati that he wanted to apologize to her, he said he knew that his apology would not heal her wounds or would not get her back her lost youth and her dreams but still he wanted her to know that he was apologetic for the way he was with her. He said he was insecure as a person and he never ever was a personable person, and Rati was always the opposite of that; she was the centre of attraction where ever she went, she always won hearts by her beauty and her nature. She was always friendly and personable and people always flocked to her and this always made him jealous and insecure. He told her that this was no reason for the way he has behaved with her but he said he could never muster up the courage to voice his problems to her or for that matter anyone and with time they only got aggravated. He said he was crushed to see her go but then he knew that there was no way he could have stopped her; he said he understood that she deserved a better life and he could never have given her that with his twisted mind and an insecure heart. He said he doesn't deserve her apology but still he is asking for it because somewhere he at least owes her that.

Rati was listening to each and everything thing he said very intently; she has never ever been a vindictive or a vengeful person but still somehow she could not bring her herself to forgive this man who has only given her sadness. He has snatched away her youth and he has brutally crushed her simple dreams of a happy family life. The only thing that was good in their relationship was her children. She knew deep down that she cannot even fake it that she has forgiven him or accepted his apology after so many years. She sat there in silence.

It was after a while that Rati conjured up the will to speak, and she realized that his expressions were frozen. He was now staring into space, his body seemed lifeless. She called for help. The doctor told her that he was dead.

Rati came back home, there was nothing more to say or do at the hospital. Her bruised past was gone. She was sitting on her couch and thinking that why was it so difficult for her to forgive him. But then she even knew the answer to her own question. Sometimes forgiveness is not enough. Words cannot heal; they cannot acknowledge a person's emotional battles. Words didn't have the power to bring back her lost youth, they didn't have the power to bring back her dreams, her hopes and her happiness, that was lost. She knew he was asking for apology because it was weighing him down but then she didn't have the will to forgive him. Even after so many years her wounds were still fresh and she still yearned for her lost youth and her crushed dreams. She didn't forgive him and she knew she has done the right thing.

Room Number 18

Sunaina was a rich and utterly spoilt brat. She was 22 and she thought that she could get everything in the world from her father's money. She was a self contained person and a narcissist to the core. She had just completed her college and now she wanted a luxurious vacation in Europe with her friends. Her father and mother were very concerned about her and they wanted her to appreciate what she had and also they wanted her to acknowledge how her parents worked their way up to this stature and money. They wanted her to know the importance of money and so both her parents told her that if she wants a vacation in Europe for two months then for a month she will have to work at an old age home her mother supported. Sunaina was in tears, thinking how can her parents do this to her, she argued a lot with them, she even tried emotional blackmailing but this time around her parents were adamant that if she wants a vacation then she has to oblige them with this job. There was absolutely no way out for her, so reluctantly she agreed.

Sunaina was also stripped off of all her luxuries and so unfortunately for her she was forced to travel like a common Mumbaikar and that meant she had to take train. They used to live in the Cuff Parade area of Mumbai and the old age home was in Dadar. So she took a train from Churchgate to Dadar and that too at 9 in the morning. It was some respite to her that she was moving against the office-hour rush but still for her all this was foreign and she totally loathed her parents for doing this to her. She got down at the Dadar station and from there she was told that it's a ten minute walk. Amidst all the chaos and hustle-bustle of everyday life, Sunaina was totally dumbstruck by this peaceful and serene old age home. She couldn't believe that it was in the centre of the city and still it was so quiet and so peaceful here. "Sandhya" was the name of the old age home and her mother has been supporting it for a long time now, and it was because of her that she got this job for a month.

Sunaina was wearing tightly fitted jeans, a low waist one at that, and a white chiffon top of Mango and she had her nails painted red as she was extremely fond of the color, and she was wearing a gloss of baby pink color and a kohl pencil to extenuate her big brown eyes. As it was day time, so she was wearing her Prada ballerinas in a nude shade. She was carrying an oversized Louis Vuitton bag and the only jewellery she wore was her Rolex watch. The woman on the reception desk looked at her in total disbelief, as if she was looking at an alien, and Sunaina could make out why, because everyone who worked here wore either Khadi or cotton. Maybe it was to beat the heat or maybe they couldn't afford designer clothes. She didn't care for what they were wearing, because it hardly mattered to her, what mattered to her was how she looked and how she presented herself; and all she wanted to do was get done with this job and hop off to Europe with all her friends.

Anita the woman on the reception desk told her to keep her bag in the locker room and then asked to attend to a certain Mr. Rajaram Deshmukh on the fourth floor and his room number was 18. She also gave Sunaina a file that contained Mr. Deshmukh's history, family and medical both. Anita showed her the locker room and also gave her a key to her locker. Sunaina stuffed her bag into the locker and headed towards the fourth floor.

She stood right in front of room number 18 and all she wanted to do was run away from here. But she understood that running away this time was not an option; so she pushed open the door and walked in to find a tiny silhouette gazing out of the window. His back was towards her and she sensed that he didn't hear her come because he was standing very still and the only sound in the room was of his heavy breathing. She walked towards him and touched him lightly on the shoulder; he turned a little abruptly at the intervention in his thoughts and a smile played on his wrinkled face. He knew all the volunteers at the old age home and she was completely new and plus she looked very different from the people who were attending him for the past 10 years.

Sunaina was in no mood to chit chat and so was he; she offered to do anything for him but he declined and he resumed his gazing at the window. She sat on the muddy brown couch in the room and opened his file. Sunaina was not much interested in reading his file but then there was nothing much to do, as even he at the moment seemed disinterested in her. Mr. Deshmukh was a retired army officer and it seemed to Sunaina he was a glorious officer back in his days. He retired in the 1970's sometime from the Indian army after serving for almost 40 years. He was blessed with two sons and now both were living abroad and his wife was long dead. Sunaina figured out that his sons and he didn't have a good rapport and maybe that is the reason he is here. He was suffering from Parkinson's and also was a severe diabetic. He's been here for almost ten years now and she was wondering how he gets by living like this; Sunaina, who was never that emotional, but she was touched at this man's apathy and his situation bothered her.

She came back next morning with some trepidation in mind; whether Mr. Deshmukh would be chatty today or would he be lost in his thoughts again for the entire day. She was a little bemused at her own self. She was wondering why he is bothering her so much; is it that she feels bad for him or is that he's the first person to have given her a cold shoulder and that was too much to handle for her. She didn't know the answer and didn't have the desire to know either. She just wanted her vacation and she just wishes that this month passes by in a jiffy.

Today as she entered Mr. D looked in good spirits and he welcomed her with a dazzling smile. Sunaina couldn't help smiling back; she had to admit he had a contagious smile. The ones that always make you smile back no matter what. He signalled her to sit besides his bed; she obeyed and sat besides his bed on a wrought iron chair. He introduced himself as Brigadier Rajaram Deshmukh and extended his hands, she shook his hands and introduced herself. He apologized to her for yesterday; he told her that yesterday was his wife's birthday and he was missing her a lot. That was the reason he was forlorn and dejected. Sunaina told him it's ok and he doesn't need to apologize, she said she understood. She was surprised that she did understand.

Now Sunaina's visits to the old age home were something she used to look forward to. Her parents too were surprised, there was one time she so vehemently objected to this job and now she so looks forward to going there and even after coming back all she can talk about is Mr. D and his friends there at the old age home. She told her mother that she was touched by their bravery; meaning to say she was surprised that how could they stay so strong emotionally, after knowing the fact that their families have disowned them and they don't want them back. Sunaina was shocked that children like that also exists who disown their own parents when parents need them the most. She never knew that few days spent with Mr. D would make her change her perspective towards life and also it made her respect her parents more. Mr. D was an angel according to Sunaina, who came into her life to teach her a lesson.

Her days used to be full of fun activity now at the old age home. Mr. D and his friends were a group of energetic old men and full of spirit. Her day used to start off with reading the Mahabharata to Mr. D and then him translating the Sanskrit shlokas for her in Hindi. Then they used to play chess and somehow he always used to beat her up at it. At one they all used to gather in the lunch room and after that used to be siesta time for all. At 3.30 there used to be tea and snacks at the game room; and a game of carom after that, where she and Mr. D always used to win. Her day used to end with a walk in the garden with Mr. D. Sunaina simply used to love walk time with Mr. D; it was in these moments that sometimes she had shared some of her most hidden feelings. She has shared her life's dreams with him and her expectations from life. Somehow it was very easy sharing these things with him; one because he was always patient with her and two he always understood her point of view. Even Mr. D had shared his misery with her; he told her once how shattered he was when his sons made him sell his house, which he had built with love and with a dream that one day they all will live together there. But he said it felt that they wanted more from life and he was fine with it; he has lived his life the he wanted to and now his sons have the right to live it the way they want to. There was just one thing he felt bad about and that was that in their dreams somewhere they completely forgot that he existed. He was not included in their lives anymore; he was an extra luggage nobody wanted. But he told Sunaina that he doesn't think much about it now; it's his life and no one has the right to control it but him. He's going to live happily and will never be bothered by trivial things. Mr. D was very fond of quoting people and his favourite was by General Eisenhower that said, never waste a minute thinking about people we should despise and forget. Then he always used to clarify that he doesn't despises his sons but he's cross with them and that's it. Mr. D used to say that after all they are his kids, his own blood and no matter what he can never bring himself to hate them, despite what they have done to him.

Days rolled by quickly and today it was Sunaina's last day and she was feeling too sad about it; a month back she never could have thought that she would cry at the mere fact that she will no longer come back to the old age home. Now her feelings were totally different and it was all because of Mr. D. He changed her and for good. Today she was taking Mr. D for a special dinner that she has promised him and she was very excited about it. Once while on their walks Mr. D has told her that he has never been to a pub and that's when Sunaina thought that on her last day she would take him to the best pub in town.

When she walked out of her room, her mother was surprised to see her all dressed in a Maharashtrian Paithani saree. She asked Sunaina what made her wear a saree..? Sunaina told her mother that Mr. D always used to tell that she looks beautiful in westerns but she would look even more beautiful in a saree; and so today she decided that she would wear a saree and surprise him. She told her mother that, Mr. D was her grandfather's age but he still became her best friend and that she would never forget him and even after she comes from Europe she would visit him there always. Both her parents were happy that they achieved what they wanted and that their daughter has finally realized that life is not just about partying and designer things but that it extends beyond it to and that is what matters the most.

Sunaina was in high spirits when she entered the old age home and waved to Anita who by now has become her friend. Anita was about to say something but before she could say anything Sunaina just walked past her and rushed to the fourth floor to room 18. She entered the room and shouted surprise!! There was no one; she wondered where Mr. D. is. Just when she was about to pick the intercom and dial Anita; Anita walked in with a manila envelope in hand and tears in her eyes. She asked Sunaina to sit down and then she told her that last night Mr. D had a massive stroke and before he could be taken to the hospital he passed away. She said his belongings are cleared now and they found this envelope addressed to her. Sunaina was stunned. She was paralysed with shock and nothing would come out of her mouth. She sat there like a lifeless doll; her expressions were frozen and even tears wouldn't come out. After it seemed like an eternity she took the envelope from Anita and she opened it with trembling hands. There was Mr. D's favourite book of quotes, a picture of him with her, his medals and a letter addressed to her. She opened the letter. He had written that he knows that he is not going to live for long now and that he has lived his life to the fullest. He has had his share of ups and downs; sorrow and happiness. He wrote he has loved every moment of his life and that he doesn't want her to cry for him. He told her that forget that he died but just remember those beautiful memories that we have shared together and always keep them alive in your heart. He told her she was a beautiful girl with substance and he wished she would live her life her own way without hurting anyone, least of all her parents. He said he would personally ask god to fulfil all her dreams and her desires; she smiled reading that, it was so quintessential Mr. D statement. He signed off writing that she made those last days of his life beautiful and that he will cherish as long as his soul remains.

For the last time she closed room 18 and walked out thinking that life is strange, it snatches away people from you who give your life a new meaning, people who give you beautiful memories, sadly become memory by a cruel stroke of fate. But she wiped off her tears as Mr. D didn't want her to cry, he had extracted that promise from her in the letter and she would fulfil that. She stood out in the garden and looked towards the fourth floor at room number 18's window; it was empty, today there was no Mr. D gazing out of it. She walked out of the old age home with beautiful memories of Mr. D, whom she will never ever forget for the rest of her life.

Re-Bonded

My phone's constant ringing woke me up on a chilly Sunday morning. I thought it was a Sunday and if the caller has nothing important to say then he or she is going to face my wrath. I mean Sunday is one day in my week when things seem normal and life takes a break from that crazy pace and lets me relax. I stretched my hands to grab hold of the damn thing and without even looking at the number I answered it. The caller on the other hand said "hey baby" and the only thought that came to my mind was that her voice hasn't changed a bit; she still had that girlish sweet voice and that peculiar way of saying "hey" with an elongated "Y". It's been over ten years since I heard her voice and hearing that made me numb inside; I wanted to respond to her but the words somehow just froze in my mouth, nothing would come out. It took me like an eternity to answer with a feeble "hello".

I said that and with the phone almost glued to my right ear I plunged into the comfort of my sheets, as if they would understand my state of mind and console me. She on the other hand was saying things, I could hardly understand her in my blurry state of mind; all I could understand was that she was coming here on Monday morning. We hung up then; I had hardly said anything to her. At the end all I could muster was see you on Monday.

Now that my sleep was completely disturbed I woke up from the bed and dragged myself to have some coffee; at the moment it was the only thing I thought would bring some sanity back. Thankfully for me my daughter Riya was having a sleepover at her aunt's place; and my husband Raghav was in Paris. I wanted time alone; I wanted time to go back in time and think about things that happened almost years ago but still they were so fresh in my mind. I set the coffee maker on and sat on the dining table and wrapped myself in the shawl. It felt like ages when finally my coffee was ready, I poured it hastily in the mug and stepped into the balcony and sat on the swing sipping.

We were a happy family, me, Mom, daddy and my elder sister Anushka. We had a decent home in Mumbai and life was perfect in our small world. I still remember daddy used to dote on me and Di; it was as if we were the centre of his universe and he just lived for us. Di and me we both used to love his puppet shows which he used to do just for us on Sundays. With puppets he used to tell us so many stories, so many poems, and songs; it's a cherished memory that we have of him and I guess it will always hold a special place in our hearts.

But I guess someone somewhere was not happy with our perfect world and I guess that's when things started going wrong. Mom and Daddy used to fight constantly; of course it was behind their locked bedroom door but still the walls were thin and used to give on them. Di and I used to crouch under the table sobbing, maybe afraid that at any moment the balloon of our happiness would burst. I was just 10 and Di was 12 when finally our balloon of happiness exploded and Mom and Daddy separated. After that his puppet shows also stopped he never did that for us again. As at that time Mom did not have any job she wasn't given our custody and in a way it made me happy. Ever since then I have only blamed her for what happened to us; over the years she tried hard to make me see things her way but I have never done that. I even stopped meeting her, the regular meeting that court had permitted her. The very look of her used to send hate waves in me, I so detested her for breaking our family. But she never gave up on me; I never ever invited her to my graduation party but she was there. I never invited her to my wedding but still she was there; she was even there in the hospital when Riya was born. She always has baffled me beyond limits. Ever since my parents broke up, the only sentiment I had nurtured for her was hate. But somehow my loathing of her or my insulting jabs at her never ever discouraged her to hate me.

I still recall 2 years back at Daddy's funeral she was there; she made herself obsolete but she was there. I remember she came and sat beside me and she just held my hands for like an hour without saying anything at all. She just held my hands in hers and sat there comforting me. Even then I had nothing to say to her, maybe we lost that mother-daughter bond somewhere years ago. I mean I did have lots of questions in mind, like why did she leave..? Or why did she abandon her family when nothing felt wrong..?

And there's lot that I want to ask her but somehow I have never mustered the courage or rather the will to ask her.

And now this sudden call from her has left me emotionally stranded once again. I came back into the present and dialled Anushka's number. She has always been in touch with Mom, so I thought I should ask her what Mom wants of me. She answered on the first ring with a breathless hello. I knew I have disturbed her power yoga time but I was not at all repentant about it. But before I could say anything, she told me that Mom's coming here to Delhi and that she is planning a road trip with me, and her. I hung up. Road trip, that sounds strange. I mean it's been years since I took any trip with Mom. I guess the last I can recall is when I was 9 and we all went to Nepal. It's been like 25 years. Oh god!! Anushka and Mom have always been in touch, but for me this was strange. I had lots of grievances to settle with her, I wanted answers to so many questions; and I guess somewhere I was a little unfair to her, I mean I never cared for her side of story and that guilt too was there. How can I face her after all that history between us..?

My Sunday just went by waltzing quickly, as if even the day was telling me that I need to clear the air with my Mom and maybe someday we will be friends.

I got up way too early on Monday; maybe I was too nervous about this whole Mom thing. In my anxiety I even woke up Riya early for school. I called up at office and told that I won't be coming as have some family emergency. Well, in a way it was a family emergency for me; meeting Mom always was something as a teenager I have detested because I hated her for breaking up the family. But I guess as I grew older, I became a little less rigid on her and many a times I tried understanding her perspective. I was restlessly sitting there on the balcony's parapet waiting for Mom's car to come by. In my nervousness I gulped down at least 7 cups of coffee since morning and I even smoked few cigarettes; I gave up on smoking long back, but today I felt the need for it to calm me down a bit.

My wait ended and I saw a car pull in front of our apartment drive-way. Mom got out of the car and pulled her sunglasses over her hair and paid the driver. She still was a knocker; I mean she was among those blessed few who never get aged. She was slender, tall and impeccably dressed as always. I heard the doorbell ring and I shot like a bullet from my resting place for the door. I opened the door and there she was smiling. She hugged me tight and gave me peck on cheeks. She collapsed on the couch and beckoned me to sit beside her.

I obeyed Mom and I guess after a long silence I asked her about her flight and also about the proposed road trip. Mom got up and she asked to fetch her some tea and breakfast as she was starving. She followed me into the kitchen and sat on the kitchen counter while I prepared some eggs and tea for her. She said, she wanted things between me and her to be fine. She wanted to rebuild that bond between us which was severed years ago. She said she knew that I hated her for breaking the family but she knew that someday I would understand her perspective and maybe forgive her for that.

The day for me rather went by too quickly. I had this impression that it will drag itself down but no it just flew away. Somehow Mom and Anushka they convinced me for the road trip; I came up with all imaginable excuses but eventually had to give in. It was arranged for Riya that she would be staying at Anushka's place with her in-laws taking care of her kids and Riya. Mom was asleep in the guest bedroom and I was lying in my room staring at the ceiling. Sleep eluded me that night, my thoughts and emotions were so jumbled up that no matter how hard I tried I couldn't sleep. Past kept visiting me all night; I finally gave up on the act of sleeping at around 4 in the morning and went to the kitchen to prepare lunch that we would carry with us on this road trip. I knew Anushka had a weak stomach and the roadside or dhaba food didn't at all agreed with her, and plus I needed something to keep my mind off the past.

It was around 8 in the morning that we started our trip to Ranikhet; me, Mom and Anushka. I was driving Raghav's range rover, as it was spacious and comfortable for this long drive. For some time there was an awkward silence between us, we all wanted to talk but the awkwardness of the past was making it a herculean task. Finally Mom broke the silence by talking. She said that we must have found her choice of destination a little odd; and yes she was right. There were memories attached to this place; no we never visited the place before but the year our parents separated, that same year we all were planning a trip to Ranikhet and of course it never materialized. And I guess after that none of us ever wanted to go there. Mom said that it was where everything ended and it was where she wanted to give it a new start.

It was around 2 in the afternoon that we crossed Rudrapur, and stopped on the outskirts of the city near a shady place to have our lunch. We all stretched and gave our legs some jerks, as it was bloody cold and we all felt that our body parts are frozen. Mom spread out a mat on the ground and we all sat there eating the lunch that I had prepared at four in the morning. I remembered Mom loved stuffed parathas, so I had prepared aloo paratha, with mint chutney, some salad, curd, and pea's pulav. Both Mom and Anushka enjoyed the meal and Mom even complimented me that I have become such a good cook. Well, I was pleased to hear that, somewhere I wanted to reconcile relations between us but at the same time was not bold enough to make the move or even forgive her for what happened. I was one confused soul.

The rest of our journey rather went by quietly, as Mom was sleeping soundly on the back seat and Anushka was busy with her book and I switched on the tape to listen to Marvin Gaye, he was a family favourite. We reached Ranikhet around 6 in the evening and it was dark there plus too cold. Mom had already made reservations at the View Hotel, so we drove up to there. She had booked a family suite and so we all were bundled into one room. I was so mesmerized by the hotel and its location. It was nestled into a beautiful scenic forest kind of area. There were huge trees around us, I guess pine mostly. It looked like a picture out of a fairly tale book. Our suite too was beautiful, and I loved it the most because it had all that antique furniture that I was so fond of. It had it all, wooden ceiling, wooden floors, antique chests and beds. I was totally in love with the place.

As we all were very tired, we freshened up and ordered something light for dinner, and after that Mom said let's take some rest and catch up in the morning. She was very tired with the road journey and she just wanted to collapse; well Anushka me and shared the same sentiment; so well slept around 9.

It must have been around 6 in the morning that I woke up; it felt as if birds were having some kind of early morning meeting just right outside our room. Our room had a veranda attached to it, so I stepped out in my Pj's just to have a look. It was still a little dark outside and those sparrows now so rare in the city were sitting in a bunch just right outside the veranda and were totally engrossed in some meeting; I guess sensing me, they called it off and flew away in haste. Mom too came out closing the door behind her, so that Anushka could sleep in peace. She took a chair beside me; it was a pregnant pause between me and Mom, we had a lot to talk to each other about but somehow we were at loss of words or maybe the right words. Finally Mom broke the silence. She said that Dad was the only man she loved but she said sometimes love is not enough for a marriage to survive. Both the partners have to cohesively work for the relationship, understand each other, be attentive to one another's needs and most importantly be non-judgemental. She said they had a love marriage and right from the beginning Dad knew about her dreams; Mom came from a theatre background and she too just like her family was in love with the stage. She was clear about it right from the very beginning. They both agreed that they'll start a family and for some years she would be at home looking after me and Anushka; and then she could work. She did keep her side of promise, she gave me and Anushka all the love and attention in the world, and she was a great mother, a good wife and an amazing homemaker. But somehow Dad forgot all about his promise to her and he became stubborn that there's no need for her to work as his income was more than enough to take care of the family. But she never wanted to work for money, theatre was her life, it was her dream. She said because of this they used be constantly at loggerheads, he never even tried to understand the fact that she too had dreams and she was ready to lead two lives; one of being a playwright and the other of being a mother and wife. But Dad never understood her or her dreams, she said somewhere he had some insecurity which he never addressed or spoke about. So finally she said she took the drastic step thinking that maybe he would nudge from his stance and look at things from her point of view but that too never happened. They got divorced and because she was unemployed at that time, our custody went to him.

Mom said that she knew somewhere I always blamed her for what happened but she was sure that one day will come when I'll try to be non-judgemental about her and think at least for a moment from her perspective. I sat there numb, for a little while I didn't know what to say to her. But then when I kept myself in her position and thought that what if Raghav wouldn't have allowed me to work, I guess I would have died. I was a journalist and I absolutely loved my work; I couldn't even fathom being without my work. And then it made sense to me, Mom just did what she felt was right for her. I mean I do understand that if you have children then you must put them first but then having children doesn't imply to the fact that you kill your dreams or bury them somewhere so deep that they seem impossible to reach out to. Never lose out on yourself while thinking about others, you may get all their love but in your own eyes you'll be a coward who never had the courage to fight for your dream.

I just got up from where I was sitting and I hugged Mom tightly, as if I didn't want her to go anywhere. I was sobbing, literally sobbing hard. I was telling her all these years I have missed having her in my life; I so badly wanted her when I got my first periods, or when I first made a boyfriend or when I got my first job. All those moments I lost out just because I never cared to bother about her perspective, she was always there for me; it was me who never reached out.

I guess hearing me and Mom crying Anushka woke up as she came out rubbing her eyes and her dishevelled hair all over her forehead. It took her sometime to register what was happening and then she too hugged me and Mom.

Well, it is said that all's well that ends well, I guess in my case I would say the end is just the beginning for me and Mom to make up for all those lost years. I have found my peace with her, we have settled the past and now all I want is a beautiful future with Mom included.

Champagne Finds Ava

1942. It is a bright sunny morning and cool summer breeze is blowing by. On the beautiful cobbled streets of Paris, Champagne is lost; roaming around aimlessly. She is tired, she is hungry, and most of all she is deprived of a place called home. A place which has been her home for the past 4 years is now just debris of ashes.

The vivid image of the house on fire is still so alive in her mind. It sent shivers down her spine. But, at the moment what worried Champagne the most is, that she doesn't want to go to that pathetic dog shelter. She has heard lurid tales about the place from one of her friend Lola who once was a resident of that place till her master took fancy on her and rescued her from that 'Dog Hell' as they all referred to it. Champagne wants a place to live; she wants a family again. She wants love again.

Champagne belonged to the Applebaum family, who lived in a small two story house on the *Rue des Rosiers*, which was essentially a Jewish quarter in Paris. The Applebaums were a simple middle class Jewish family, consisting of Mrs. Applebaum and Mr Applebaum and the senior Mrs. Applebaum; and they were the residents of this area for years now and they ran a bakery shop, which was doing good. Four days back, a drunk German soldier, who by the way was on a self- deployed mission of destroying the Jewish people, burnt their house at night and by the time the Applebaums realized that the house was on fire, things were beyond control; realizing this the senior Mrs. Applebaum threw Champagne in the garden so that she survives. Champagne had tears in her eyes when she saw her house burned down to ashes and all her three masters dead. Her heart was broken and filled with grief. She left the place and it's been four days now that Champagne is still wandering around aimlessly around the streets of Paris. She is lost, she is sad, and she is a little frightened.

Its waging war in Europe and the rest of the world, but Champagne's only worry is how to find food and water. Tired of her attempts to get food for herself, Champagne finds her way to the park and is just lying in the shade of a tree when she suddenly sees the most beautiful little girl she has ever seen, sitting on a chair and watching other kids having fun around her. For some unknown reason, Champagne just couldn't keep her eyes off the little girl; she had chestnut brown hair and a milky white complexion and the most beautiful part of the little girl were her beautiful emerald green eyes. But Champagne also saw sadness in those big beautiful eyes. All Champagne wanted to do was to go and cuddle the little girl and ask her, "What's bothering you little girl..? Champagne's here for you.. ☺"

Well, apparently the little girl's time for playing or rather watch other kids play was over and she was being ushered by a stern looking woman with a very sombre expression on her face. Just at the same time Champagne was running for her life, as two big bully dogs were chasing her as she was trespassing in their territory and they wanted her out. All of a sudden while this chase, Champagne collides with a car and is left unconscious.

To Champagne it felt like an eternity, it felt like a lifetime has passed away, when she slowly lifted her eyes and saw that beautiful little girl looking at her so lovingly. Champagne was lost in those big doleful eyes. She was so lost that she even missed out on that little girl talking to her and consoling that she's going to be fine.

Ava was born to a beautiful family in Paris but tragedy stuck and she lost both her parents in a cruel car crash an year back and also lost her legs in that brutal accident. After the accident, Ava was taken in by her maternal grand-mother. They always have stuck a cord and their relationship went along famously but still when all alone, Ava used to miss her Mama and Pa and used to pray to God to either send them back or let her go to them. She was lost and miserable without them. Ava did not have any friends, as kids her age used to find her boring, because they failed to understand her condition and her apathy. Ava was lonely and friendless. Her Grana, as she fondly used to refer to her, did everything possible to make the little girl happy as she used to be, but failed.

Now, somewhere up above in heaven, God was really moved by the tragedies in both Ava and Champagne's life. He made a plan. He created those tragedies, so it was his turn as well as his duty to do some damage control, and which is something God always does. The plan was to create a situation where Champagne was to find Ava, so that they could be friends and give solace and love to each other; something which was badly and really missing from both of their lives. He sent two of his best angels, Grace and Beauty in the form of bully dogs to chase Champagne. Champagne was too terrified of those bullies and was running for her life, when she collided badly with Ava's car. After this moment, the whole life changed for Ava and Champagne.

Ava's Grana was allergic to dogs but after seeing her grand-daughter's happiness and her smile back, she happily ignored it and welcomed Champagne with open arms. Though Mrs. Smith, Ava's governess, was still against the idea of an unknown strange dog staying in the house but who cared.

Grana was happy as Ava was ecstatic with her canine companion, and well for Champagne her whole world revolved around Ava. They shared their bedroom, they even shared their toys. Champagne was Ava's 24 hour companion, something she simply loved doing. Ava now used to proudly take Champagne with her to the park and wait not just to watch the other kids play, but she herself used to play with her little canine bestie. They loved playing ball, and hide-n-seek, and Champagne and Ava especially used to love the part of hiding from the domineering Mrs. Smith.

In just a matter of a few days, Ava and Champagne became inseparable. Coming in of Champagne in Ava's life changed her whole attitude towards life, and she became a more positive and a happy person. Smile and happiness were back in little Ava's life and all the credit for this went to our little cherubic Champagne (Who was God's gift to Ava).

Sometimes tragedies in life makes us meet people or in Ava's case animals and they give a new meaning to our life and bring back all the forgotten happiness and smile back in life.

So, whenever something happens, it very definitely happens for a reason and the reason is always revealed it's just that you need to go out find it and find your happiness again.

Dogs indeed are a man's best friend. Though they cannot speak our language, they shower us with their love. Love is a universal language and is understood by every living organism on the planet earth. Always be kind and loving towards the animals. They love us unconditionally, and they really do. So, let's be kind towards them and give our unconditional love to them.

House On The Hill

My name is Nalini and I live with my family in Nainital. It's a small town on the hills and except for admiring nature there's nothing much to do here. The story of my life is not extraordinary but something happened one night and it made my life beautiful. It gave a new meaning to my existence and it made me felt loved. Let me tell you my little story.

I was born in a family which was small but there was no dearth for love. My mother was a teacher at the prestigious school in Nainital and my father owned a hotel. Life was perfect for all of us. But for me life changed completely that fateful night when while returning home after watching a play, our car was hit by a speeding truck and in that accident I lost my mother. I have always heard people say that it could take minutes for a person's life to change and for me it was really true; that accident changed my whole life. I was just ten at that time but even then I understood that my loss is something that will never ever be compensated for. My father got married once again and I won't say that my step-mother is a bad person, she is okay but then she is not my mother. It's been two years now since my mother has passed away and earlier we used to live in the quarters provided by my mother's school but after her demise we had to vacate that and now we have moved to a new place.

The place where we live is near to the lake which Nainital is known for and from our garden there's a beautiful view of the hills all around us and somewhere on that hill is a house, standing there in all its past glory and its beautiful Victorian architecture. All my friends say that the house is haunted and an evil looking lady lives there and she roams around in the night; they say they have never ever seen her venture out in broad daylight and that confirms their belief all the more that she is a spirit or maybe a vampire. I have never believed in ghosts and that's what one day made me go to that house in the afternoon. The road or rather the small trail that leads to the house was beautiful; it presented a serene picture of the valley down there and also gave a panoramic view of the lake. It had many winding turns and the trail on both the sides was covered with thick pine and Deodar trees. It was a tiring trek till the house but when I reached there, I thought it was worth it. My friends got distracted by their hunger midway through the trek and so they stopped for lunch. But I was so enthused that I told them that I won't stop for lunch and so I continued my sojourn upwards.

The moment I reached the end of the trial there was a wooden board nailed to the road that said, "Private property". There was a huge wrought iron gate, like the ones shown in the movies. The house that stood there was in one word magnificent. I have never ever seen a beautiful house like that and it just took my breath away. From down there the view of the house was not at all clear and for obvious reasons. The house was a red brick structure and it had four huge columns on both its sides. It also had a sit-out on both sides with French doors. The main door of the house was a beautiful one with a brass knocker. It was a beautiful two – storey house and in no way it looked haunted to me. The garden around the house was splendid too. It had walnut trees, pine trees, deodar trees and it also had a huge oak tree which looked at least two hundred year old. I was standing there admiring the beauty when I saw a vision on the first floor window. I felt as if when I was admiring the beauty of the house and its surroundings, someone was watching me. But when I looked up there who ever was watching me backed off. The strangest part of the entire house was that it had no guards. My friends eventually having made the trek walked up to the house and even they were mesmerized by the sheer elegance of the red brick structure and its imposing austerity. It was getting late and in sometime it would be sunset and thus we were forced to go back.

It was after dinner when everyone was asleep in my house that I huddled myself in a jacket covered my head with a muffler and took out my torch. I sneaked out of the back door and took the trial that lead to the house on the hills once again. It was 11 in the night and it seemed the whole town was sound sleep and everyone was loitering their time in dreamland till sunrise. There's not much to do on the hills and so everyone goes to sleep early, as even our day's start earlier than the people living in other cities. It worked in my favour as there was no one to stop me from going up there.

The trail that leads to the house was beautiful in the morning but at night it wore an altogether different look. The moon light was mystifying everything around here and the sounds that the cricket were making were invoking fear in me somehow; as if they were telling me to go and not venture out further. I finally made my way up there and once again I was standing right in front of those imposing wrought iron gates. This time around I mustered up all the courage I had in me and silently flung open the gates. I walked up to the house and now I was standing right in front of its beautiful door with a brass knocker. I was standing there lost in my thoughts on what should my next move be; it was just when I was contemplating my next move that the door opened and I stood there frozen.

I must have fainted because when I woke up I found myself lying on a four poster bed and I saw a woman whose back was facing me at the moment. She turned around and smiled at me. She came and sat beside me on the bed; she was smiling and was lovingly stroking my forehead. Now that she was so near to me she didn't feel or look scary. I was trying to find the right words to say to her but at that moment nothing came to mind. My mother always used to say that I was good with words but somehow at the moment I was completely at loss. I knew I have made a fool of myself and also that I have hurt her feelings by fainting like this.

She got up again fetched me a glass of warm milk. She asked me drink it. Her voice was melodious; it was sweet-toned and it had this lyrical beauty to it. She told me her name was Felicity and that she was a widow. She said she has been living here since almost 25 years. I somehow managed to utter my name to her and then I asked her something which for a moment she was surprised to hear but then she gave a little chuckle and answered my question.

She said 20 years back there was an accident in the kitchen which caused a huge fire which took her husband's life away and it also ruined her face forever as well as her life.

She walked to the window and opened it; a draft of cold breeze came in. She turned around and said that she and her husband had a love marriage and they both were very happy together. On that fateful day it was their fifth anniversary. She said she was expecting too and was eager to share that good news with her husband during the dinner but then that dreadful fire blew away all the happiness she had in the world. But then the worst was not over she even lost her child. It's been twenty years since that accident and her wounds are still fresh and the memories of that fateful day still haunt her. I asked her why she never ventures out and I also told her that people think she is a ghost. She laughed and then she said that people used to cringe at her because she had those horrible burn marks on her face and that is the reason she refrains from going out. It's only in the night when the whole town is sleeping that she steps out because then no one sees her.

I told her that she doesn't need people's approval; it's her life and she has been through a traumatic experience and if they don't understand that then it's their problem not her. I then told her that two years back I lost my mother and for a few months the only thought that I was occupied with was to end my life and go to my mother. But then that would have been unfair on my part; my mother always used to say that when we are born we are allotted a particular time on earth and we should use that time to make our and everyone's life happy. She always used to say that we get to live once and that once should be made worthwhile.

I really don't know what effect my speech had on her but she came to me and hugged me tight. It was then that a bond formed between us and it was the beginning of our lifelong friendship. It's said that love unites people, strangely in our case it was not just love but also our sorrows that united us. I really don't want to know what exactly brought us close but I am happy that she came into my life and made it worthwhile and beautiful again. I guess somewhere even I did the same to her. To her I was the child she never had and that was the reason she showered me with unconditional love.

Epilogue

I'm now 27 years old and I live in Delhi and am happily married. I am going to Nainital today as its Aunt Felicity's birthday and I know she would be eagerly waiting for me. She's old now and is restricted to a wheel chair but the one thing that hasn't changed a bit about her is her benevolent smile. The house is still the same though a little faded now with time but it still casts that magical spell on me every time I go there. That night years ago changed our lives and gave a new meaning and I'll always be so grateful to god for that.

My Fat Life

Part I

The alarm clock was ringing insistently as if in some vindictive way it just wanted to throw me out of the bed; but eventually it won and I had to get up. Like everyone else all across the world, even I hated Mondays; they were cruel. But little did I know that this Monday was going to be the best in my life and that it would change the way I used to think about life. Well, my name is Revati and I am 25 years old and I work for a news channel. I completed my degree in journalism from a reputed college here in Delhi and now I work as their junior editor. I was born and raised in Delhi and the one thing that I really love about Delhi except of course for my family is food; Delhi's food is just out of this world and I am a complete foodie and well that is very apparent when you see me; I'm curvaceous and slightly overweight. All through my school life and the entire college life I was a misfit in groups; umm, no don't get me wrong, I have friends and we all have been together ever since I guess kindergarten but apart from my close knit group of friends I don't have other friends. Not that

I regret that but sometimes I used to feel bad that how can people judge you that you are not cool just because you are a little overweight than others; that's not right.

Everyone at the office was okay, I mean we all are so stacked up with work that sometimes it gets difficult to even take your eyes off the computer and relax. I was at my desk when a person without even asking for my permission came and sat on the chair opposite to mine. I was heads down in work and literally heads down and just with a wave of hand I told him I'm busy please come later. But he seemed like a hard nut to crack, he told me he can wait. The moment I heard his voice something happened; I mean something filmy happened in my head, I could hear drums and guitar playing at the same time. He had a deep husky voice and a slight British accent which was very sexy. The moment I heard the voice I knew that it was the sexy new guy in office, which everyone was talking about. He's joined our channel almost four months back and ever since he's been here all everyone could talk about was him. He's not that regular 10 on 10 sexy but he's sexy in a very unconventional way, he's got grey matter intact unlike some men I have lately come across and he's too good at presenting news and also grilling the politicians on a talk show he hosts. He was earlier with some international news conglomerate but then in just whimsical manner he decided that he wanted to go back to his country and work there. So, viola!! He came to work with us.

Ever since he has joined I have been secretly admiring him but not openly unlike other girls I have not done that; you must be wondering for the reason, well it's simple, look at me. I mean who wants to go out with a girl like me, I am overweight, I wear flats, most of the time my hair is tied up in a chignon knot and I never ever apply make-up. To sum up in one word, I am a plain Jane and why would a guy like him be interested in someone like me. I was so lost in my thoughts that I completely forgot that he was sitting there; I came back to senses and in a very cool manner I asked him what is it that he wanted from me; it sounded strange to my ears because in my head there were so many instruments playing at the same time and my stomach seemed full with butterflies. Now you are absolutely not going to believe what he said; he asked me out for coffee. For a moment I thought he's crazy and he should be put in an asylum. I mean me.? I was dumbfounded and I just sat silently staring at him, as if I didn't understand what he said. He literally shook me by the arm to pull me out of my trance. I wanted to ask him so many questions and wanted to say witty things too but none came out of my mouth. All I could do was nod my head in silent approval. I felt like dancing like crazy in my office cubicle. I mean, Nirad Bannerjee was asking me out was so uncalled for, I mean in a good way.

Part II

It's been a year of our first coffee date and now I have so many that I have lost count of it. The year went by so beautifully and it was all because of Nirad. You know the very first thing that I asked him when we went out for coffee the first time; I simply asked him why me.? And he simply replied why not. I told him I wanted more than that and it was then that he told me the most beautiful thing anyone has ever said to me. He said that he has never ever yearned for fashion mannequin kind of women; he has always wanted women with substance, and women who would be realistic about the way they look and not obsessed with their wardrobe, their hair or their make-up. He said women of all kinds are beautiful, according to him it's insane and totally disgusting to judge someone by the way they look or by their weight. Nirad told me that everyone is different for a reason and one should love that uniqueness and not judge people based on looks or weight; they don't count. He said no one is perfect, not even a women with a size zero figure and a porcelain complexion; everyone is flawed and everyone have their imperfections and you just need to embrace them and move one. Never get those trivial issues get you down or lose faith in yourself. He told me how you look like or rather what's your weight they don't count; make use of your talent and contribute beautiful things to the world. He told me lastly that love yourself and the people around you will realize your worth by themselves. You don't want to starve yourself or go on crazy fruit diet just to please someone or just to fit in.

Those few minutes just changed me completely and for good. I am not saying one should not be thin but if one is not then they should not be discouraged by that or people should not judge them by the way their weight is.

Well, Nirad and I are officially dating; at the moment I don't know where we are heading but I love the place I am in right now. Umm, by the way I have started a healthy regime for myself and I love every bit of my life now. I just want to say one thing, love your curves, because for others to love you, you need to love yourself first and this is the most important lesson my relationship has taught me.

=()=

The Candy Floss Man

I was in class four; it's been since then that I have developed an immense liking for candy floss and the man who use to sell it. It was a daily ritual for all of my friends. In our second recess we used to rush out of the school for that 2 rupee candy floss. We all used to save our weekly allowance for the candy floss treat every day. Now when I think of it I really don't know why we all had such fascination for candy floss; maybe because as kids those bright colors used to attract us or I guess the man who used to sell it or maybe his decrepit cycle on which he used to carry that yummy candy floss. He was an interesting person to be around always and he was full of stories for us every time. He was also very generous, sometimes when we had cash crunch he used to give all of us free candy floss. We never ever paid any heed whatsoever to the loss he might have to incur because of this generous gesture. There was also more one thing about him which no one could have ignored and that was his smile. Well, I'll agree his teeth were tobacco stained and some were missing too; but he had one of those contagious smiles which always make you smile back no matter what. His big brown eyes used to twinkle with sheer joy seeing all of us eating candy floss and sharing our tales with him. There was also one more astonishing fact about him; no matter what the weather used to be, he was always there selling that eye catching candy floss. The weather could never ever dampen his spirit.

I still can recall how he looked; he was a tall man and he was old. He didn't have one arm. He always used to tell us that he was a soldier in the army and in one battle he lost his arm and thus he was forced by circumstances to retire. We never knew his name and thus we all used to call him Baba. For many years to come that was all we knew about him, till that day when me and a friend of mine went to find his house because it was a week that he wasn't there selling candy floss and that got us a bit concerned.

Finding his house was a big challenge for us and after asking the other hawkers around the school we were finally able to fetch the address for his house. It was not that far from school, so we decided to walk. The road that leads to his house was very narrow and kind of derelict; as if it's been long since anyone has paid attention to the road or the people who used to live in those small miniature dwellings. It was a little depressing walk till his place.

Finally for us the harrowing walk came to an end and now we were standing right in front of Baba's house. It was not difficult to locate his house; his decrepit bicycle was standing right outside the house with some deflated packets of candy floss. The door was locked and so we knocked on it. We stood there for good ten minutes but still there was no answer. We knocked again and this time we could hear some rustling sound coming from inside the house.

Eventually the door flung open and Baba was standing there right in front of us and he was looking too tired and sick. His eyes wore a woebegone look and there was an air of despondency around him. After opening the door for us he somehow managed to crawl into bed again and because of all this walking his breathing became a little too heavy. We were crestfallen looking at him in this condition and we wanted to do something for him that would make him feel good and would elate his deflated spirit. I touched him on his forehead, he was burning with fever. We asked him that we can call our parents and they would take him to the doctor but he refused. He said that he'll be fine it's just fever. He said he was a soldier and a mere fever cannot defeat him. His nonchalant attitude towards illness was not liked by both of us. We offered to make him some tea and food but he said there was nothing in the house. He said his pension was not enough to sustain him and thus he was forced to sell candy floss and now due to his illness he was unable to do that. We felt bad for him; my friend even offered him his weekly allowance but Baba was not comfortable taking money from us or our parents.

For a while it seemed as if all three of us have reached an impasse; but then Baba seeing our eagerness to help him came up with an idea. Listening to his idea we both felt happy and relieved that finally we would be able to do something for him; also that would in no way hurt his self-respect. Both I and my friend agreed with Baba on his idea of taking our help and the idea was selling his candy floss for a few days till he was fine. Right after school we both used to rush to his house to make candy floss. Then we used to stand outside other schools and colleges to sell it and eventually by the evening we used to return back to Baba's house with the days collection and we used to make dinner for him. This went on till almost ten days.

It was our short recess again and we all rushed out for our favourite candy floss. We were very happy to see Baba standing there with the most attractive looking candy floss on his cycle and with his quintessential smile.

Epilogue

Sometimes those small and to us insignificant gestures could change someone's life and bring smile on their face. Life is all about making everyone happy and if for that we have to walk an extra mile I guess it should not be a bother.

Irsia

It was almost 11 in the night, and Rustom was getting
restless. He was pacing up and down the shop, and was
constantly twitching his moustaches. Even the aroma of
home brewed coffee couldn't bring him to sit down and relax.
His mind was flooded with so many thoughts at the same
time, and none of them made sense to him.

Every night at 9, Irsia used to come to the bakery to get
brown bread and croissants. In the past six months, she has
never been late. Today she was almost two hours late, and
it got Rustom a little worried. Well, Rustom had a thing for
Irsia. Actually, not just a thing, but he was head over heels
in love with her, and he just didn't have the courage to say
that to her. Every morning in front of the mirror, with a lily in
his hands, he used to practice the lines he would say to Irsia.
But, his words would just freeze in his mouth the moment he
would see her walk in to his shop. Rustom's assistant Philip
used to call the day off at around 7, and after that it used to
be only Rustom at the shop. Once, out of curiosity, Philip
stayed back to get a glimpse of Irsia, but strangely that day

she didn't come. Most of Rustom's friends believed that he was making up stories and there was no woman called Irsia.

Irsia was a very beautiful woman. Her skin was like white porcelain and it complemented her unusually big dove like purple eyes. She had an aquiline nose, fuller lips and high cheek bones. Her hair was the color of chestnut, and she was always very experimental with her hairdos. She was tall and she had a curvaceous body. She told Rustom that she has newly moved to the neighbourhood. She was a daily customer at Rustom's bakery for the past six months. Adrenalin used to rush through his body the moment he used to see her walk in every night.

Dejectedly, today Rustom closed his bakery for the day and he started walking towards his apartment. He lived nearby and he always used to prefer walking. Today, just like his mood, even the weather was stormy. It was very windy, and Rustom predicted that soon there'll be showers.

Rustom somehow felt that there must have been something wrong and that's the reason Irsia has not showed up at the shop; he thought she was new in the area and she didn't know many people here and he felt it was his duty to help her if she needed it. He made up his mind and started walking towards her apartment. He knew where she stayed, he remembered she once mentioned that her building was one of the oldest one in area.

By the time he reached her apartment, it was raining hard. Rustom looked at the old and kind of dilapidated structure of the building where she lived; he smiled that it was indeed too old and it need revamping badly. He was not aware about her apartment number and so he walked towards the wall where the names of owners of the flats were listed. He spotted her number; her apartment was on the sixth floor. As there was no elevator, he took stairs. Rustom was only 50 years old, but age was dawning on him a bit too early; by the time he reached her floor he was panting for breath badly. He took support of the banister and was standing still just to catch up on his breath. He didn't want her to see him like this at all.

After a while, he rang the doorbell. It was loud; the ones that made you irk or cringe. He was about to turn around and go; it was just then that Irsia opened the door with her bewitching smile. She flung opened the door and invited him in. It was like - he was mesmerized by her, and followed her like a puppy dog inside her apartment. He left his umbrella outside the apartment. He was so smitten by her at that time that he didn't even notice the other umbrellas lined up there. Irsia closed the door.

Epilogue

In the morning Mrs. Smith was stepping out for her morning walk and it was just then that she noticed another umbrella outside the apartment of deceased Irsia Contractor.

Suman

It was a windy and a cold morning in Delhi. Suman sat there huddled in a shawl with her old and worn out trunk at the Delhi railway station. She was waiting for her train to arrive that would take her back to Mumbai. Suman had come to Delhi with lot of hopes; she wanted to spend time with her grand children, she now wanted to live with her son Mahesh, as she was getting old and she used to be sick most of the times; she wanted care and protection of a family. With all these hopes and dreams she came to Delhi. Mahesh was working as a General Manager with a big private company and even his wife was working as a lecturer. Mahesh was now 40 years old and he was Suman's only son. She just had Mahesh to call her family in this whole wide world. There was an announcement at the station that her train is 1 hour late. With a lot of struggle she got up and fetched herself tea and some rusk, and with that she sat again near her trunk and was lost, thinking about the days that were gone, the years that have passed.

Suman was a very bright 16 year old girl and she always topped in her class; both her father and mother were very proud of their only daughter. Her father Pandurang Ghorpade was a foreman at the mill and her mother Sumitra used to stitch clothes. They lived in a rented room in a chawl in the Kalbadevi area of Mumbai. They had less but they were content with whatever they had. Suman recalled that everything was going fine for them, until that strike at her father's mill. All the workers were protesting against the mill owners; they were being instigated by the union leader Sundar; Pandurang knew about it and despite the protest from other workers he showed up at work, because for him work was worship and he had no complaints with his owners. Seeing Pandurang show up at work despite admonitions from Sundar, he was beaten up badly and was thrown at the chawl gates by Sundar's men. Suman remembers her Baba as she fondly used to call him, was badly injured and his whole body was covered in blood. No one in the chawl stepped up to help them and she and her mother took him to the nearby hospital. On arrival at the hospital he was declared dead, as the doctor said that he had several head injuries and there was internal bleeding too. For Suman and her mother, the world came to a standstill. They sat there on the floor in complete silence; their whole world has come crumbling down after her father's death and she and her mother did not have a clue how to go forward from here. Suman remembers that the days that followed her father's death were blurry and she felt as if she did everything in a state of daze.

It had been a month since her Baba passed away; life was getting back to some normalcy for them; but for Suman more bad news was in store. It was in the evening her mother was going to deliver clothes at a shop for which she used to stitch sometimes, it was alteration work; while going to the shop her mother was hit by a speeding car and she was killed in an instant. When the news reached Suman that her mother has met with an accident and was killed, she just fainted. The rest of the days again went in a daze for her as she was really scared and she knew that she had completely no one to turn to or call family. Her mother had been an orphan was raised in an orphanage and her father was the only son and his parents passed away when Suman was born. She was told by the landlord to vacate the apartment as her rent was due and he knew that there was no way she could pay for it. So at the age of 16 Suman was orphaned and had no place to call home. She even left school and tried doing different jobs to sustain her but in vain. Six months passed since her parents died and still Suman was sleeping on the streets with no good work. No one was interested in giving work to an orphan girl. It was during this time that she came across Rajjo. Once while trying to clean the windows of the cars that used to stop at the signal, Rajjo spotted Suman and asked her to come with her, she promised Suman that she would give her work and also a place to live. Suman readily agreed and got in the car with Rajjo. That was the biggest mistake she made in her life but then there was no coming back. Rajjo used to run a brothel and she had many young and innocent girls working for her. Suman was very beautiful and at the age of 16 had a full figure and that caught Rajjo's attention; she too became a victim of Rajjo.

Over the years that Suman used to work for Rajjo, she tried to run but in vain and in the end she gave up. It was here at Rajjo's brothel that Suman got pregnant and at a very later stage she came to know about it, and she decided that she will have this baby, as she wanted someone to call her a family. The brothel was a four storey building and the living quarters for the girls were on the third and fourth floor. Mahesh grew up there amidst the other women, but Suman made a vow that she would educate her child and would give him a college education so that he wouldn't be forced to live in this hell and maybe someday he would give Suman a home and she thought that in her final days she would be with her son and his family. Her dreams did come true, Mahesh was a bright student and he excelled in school as well as in college. After his graduation he landed a job in Delhi; before leaving for Delhi he promised Suman that the moment he settles there he would call her there. That time never came, somewhere Suman was anticipating this. Even in his school and college days, he used to be embarrassed talking about his mother. He never ever even introduced her to any of his friends.

He was 22 when he left Mumbai and it's been 18 years since he even met Suman. He used to send her some money and that was the only connection she had with her son. Suman was old now and it's been years since she stopped working and now she used to live in a small room in a chawl. She had some foreboding before she decided to go to Delhi to stay with her son and his family but she thought maybe all these years must have melted his heart a little and maybe he could let his mother stay with him in her final days. But Suman was wrong; the moment she reached his home in Delhi, just on the door step he told her to go away and not to bother him and his family. He stuffed some money in her palms and told her to leave; his wife called out to him asking who was at the door and his answer made Suman cry. He told his wife that an old beggar woman has come. Hearing herself being referred as an old beggar woman, made Suman cry; she couldn't believe that her son for whom she did everything she could to make his life comfortable, had disowned her. She felt alone and dejected, her tears wouldn't stop thinking that her son was ashamed of calling her his mother. He was ashamed of her profession, but he did not know that Suman too was embarrassed about it but she had no other choice. The announcement at the railway station brought her back to the present. She lifted her trunk and boarded the train to Mumbai.

It was after a year that Mahesh received a courier; he opened it and sat there in complete silence, a teardrop rolled down his eye. The courier was from Mumbai, it had all his mark sheets, his medals, his old toys, his collection of cassettes, his marbles, and all his batman comics. There was also a small box which had his mother's jewellery, which was a ring and a pair of bangles and along with it was a letter. He opened it, it was from his mother. She started it by giving him blessings and she wrote that she wished him all the luck and also she wished all the luck for his wife and the kids. She apologized to him that she was an embarrassment to him all her life and she said she wished he had a decent family and a good mother. She wrote that she is dying and maybe by the time he receives the courier she would be dead. She gave him many blessings and loads of love for everyone in the family. And lastly she wrote that it was not by choice she opted for this profession but it was the only way out for her to survive. She asked him not to judge her harshly. For Mahesh it felt as if a lifetime has passed, while sitting there with all that his mother has sent and reading her letter. He felt rotten and he knew all his life he will have to live with this feeling. He safely packed all the things his mother has sent in a trunk and he took the letter and kept it in his safe. He prayed to his mother to forgive him, he knew it was the least he could do. He has been a rotten son and now there was no way he could make up for it. Sometimes we learn lessons in life a hard way.

The Memory Never Fades

It's been two months since Aji (Grandmother) passed away. I lost my parents when I was just four years old, they were going back to Pune after spending time in Mumbai with Aji and on the highway they were met with a terrible accident. I was taken in by my mother's mom, that's Aji. My father's parents passed a long time back and he just had a sister. She was married with children and she couldn't afford to keep yet another one and so I was taken by Aji. At four you don't have that vivid a memory of your parents and so for me the transition was a little easy.

My Aji was a little old fashioned in her beliefs; she used to believe a lot in the reincarnation thing and she firmly used to believe that I was her sister who passed away the same day my mother conceived me. Well, I have never believed in all that but she was very sure about it and I guess it's because of that reason that she loved me doubly; well one as her granddaughter and the other as her sister. Whatever it was she loved me deeply and so did I. She had a small one bedroom hall kitchen apartment in Dadar, she used to really take pride in her home, my Ajoba (grandfather) had put all his savings into this and it was their little paradise, a dream home in this bustling metropolis where everyone comes with a dream of making a dream home someday. He passed away when I was two, so I have no memories of him. Aji gets his pension and I inherited my parent's savings, so it was a little tight string budget for us but we managed beautifully. I still remember she used to get beautiful dress for me on every Gudi-Padwa (its Maharashtrian new year), though the budget was low string but Aji never made me realize that. She used to make me get up early in the morning, shower and eat neem leaves, well it's our ritual; it's said that it purifies our body's immune system for any diseases. I still recall all my friends used to be at my place to eat her Dadar famous Puran poli and Shrikhand. Aji always used to say "It's New Year Ila and we must welcome it with arms wide open, and there should be no stinginess on New Year's." Both Aji and me we used to make beautiful rangoli on the New Year's Day at our door step with vibrant colors.

Years passed by quickly for us. Aji made my childhood so beautiful that I never realized that I was an orphan. I completed my college, I did masters in Sanskrit and right after college I got an offer to work at the same college I studied from. Aji was ecstatic that day, her happiness knew no bounds, she kept saying all day to everyone "My Ila is a professor now, I am so proud of her, no one ever did that you know in the family. But then Ila was always an exceptional child." Well Aji was like that, she took pride in everything that I did. She always made me feel special.

I opened the door to her flat and was greeted by a faint rusty smell of a place which hasn't been inhabited in a while.

The low sofa and its matching chairs were beckoning me to come and sit. The walls were painted in the faintest shade of yellow, Aji's favourite. Seeing that it so reminded me of Aji; I was overwhelmed with nostalgia. She used to sit there often after doing all her chores. She was very fond of the Indian style low baithak. There were a lot of colourful cushions on the sofa and also on the chairs. I sat there and touched the fabric fondly and again went back in time when I was in school; Aji used to make me sit on the sofa with her and do the home work there rather than in the bedroom, while she used to read Ramcharitmanas. Our main door used to be locked only during the night, otherwise all day long it used to be open, Aji was a chatter box, always full of fun stories and anecdotes; she was friends with everyone in the apartment building. I can hardly remember the time when I used to come back from school and there was no one there. She was a gregarious woman; always smiling and making everyone smile.

I came back to the present; it was no use raking up all the memories, they would only make me a weaker person and that Aji would never want me to be. Though the house wore a little rusty smell but still there was this faint smell of coconut oil in the air, it again reminded me of Aji. She always applied coconut oil in her hair, and even at 75 years of age her hair was black and thick. Aji was a little over 5 feet in height and she was as fair as the moon. She had huge charcoal black eyes and perfectly arched eyebrows and that too without ever stepping in to a beauty parlour. I always used to tease her that she must have been a knocker in her hay days and Aji always used to scold me for that, "Why do you keep saying such things Ila." I have always seen her wearing a saree even at night. She never ever wore anything else; sometimes I used to wonder was Aji born in a saree too. Aji was fond of cotton sarees and Paithani sarees also but only for special occasions; like she wore a beautiful red and yellow Paithani on my wedding day. To be honest she was looking more beautiful than me, though she never agreed but she was. Her dazzling smile, her honest nature, her love, her concern everything made her the most beautiful woman ever.

Aji was deeply religious all her life and I guess that is the reason she even went away in peace. She had a stroke in her sleep, she never woke up. The news of Aji's demise left me paralyzed emotionally. I didn't know how to react. I lost my parents when I was just four and after that she became my world. Everything revolved around her for me; she became the epicentre of my universe. She was not just my Aji but she was even my best friend. On so many nights I have slept on her lap and poured out my heart and she has always very patiently listened to everything I had said and has always offered me solutions to all my problems. How can she leave me and go away. It was not fair. I never even got to say goodbye to her properly. There were no last words from her. Even now when I close my eyes, I see her round face, those huge charcoal eyes, and that sweet lullaby voice asking me "Ila is everything fine with you, if no then always remember that Aji is here."

Everyone was asking me to sell the flat but I could never bring myself to selling it. Selling the flat would be like selling away Aji's memories forever and I could never ever do that. Ratnakar my husband said, Ila do what you think is right, do not listen to what everyone says.

I did would do what is right for me; I never would sell this flat, it was Aji's last remembrance for me and her memory still lingers here. Her coconut hair oil and her mogra perfume everything lingers and reminds me of her. I can never sell off her memory to someone else. I wouldn't cling on to it, as I have my life to live but at least when I am down and I need a place to sort out things I know where I'll find peace; it's at Aji's. And as it's said that it's hard to forget someone that you know you'll always remember.

The Wrong Number

The whole apartment was engulfed in darkness; outside it was raining heavily. The dull thuds of rain water on the terrace and the lashing winds were a constant reminder of the storm that was building up inside his head. At just the age of 36, Mukul felt that his whole world has collapsed in just one go and now there was nothing left for him. To him his life now felt like an abyss; his heart was a bottomless void, devoid of any feelings or emotions. He had made himself a drink and he emptied the bottle of sleeping pills in it, now all he wanted was to muster up the courage to gulp it down and wait for death to engulf him; at-least that would be a respite.

It's been an hour and even now Mukul's hands are shaking when he tries to hold the glass. His whole being is trembling, he is confused, in a dilemma; he so wants to embrace death but yet as is the story of his life, courage is missing. He throws himself in the rocking chair and its motion which once was a soothing balm to him, now is only aggravating his uneasiness and his frustration.

Mukul could hear a constant shrill ring of the phone; he couldn't make out whether it was ringing actually or was it just a dream. After several seconds he wakes up from the dull slumber which he crawled into and he picks up the phone; his motive was to slam the phone down, gulp the drink and die, but somehow the voice on the other hand, made him bring the receiver to his ears and listen.

Her voice was like a cascading flow of water, not in a river or sea but in a spring or a lake. It's soft gushing sounds, its flowery sweetness, the sweet warmth of her voice; it sounded like a lullaby and he didn't want her to stop. He was lost in her voice, it felt as if all his worries and the burden that he has been carrying for a while have been rendered moot by the melodious tilt in her voice. It felt like ages that he came out of that trance and he focused on what she was trying to say. She was asking for some Mukul Dasgupta, and she repeated his number too; there was just a two digit difference between his number and the other guy's number and he thought that's the reason for this call or rather the confusion he sensed in her voice. He wanted to tell her that he's not Mukul Dasgupta but he's Mukul Mitra, but somehow his feelings at the moment were so overwhelming that he couldn't utter a word.

She was about to hang up because there so no response except for the heavy breathing sound that penetrated through the receiver. At the other end Mukul started to sob, his sobs became uncontrollable and that made her hang on to the phone. She felt as if he was totally broken and she wanted to know the reason why, what has happened that he cannot control his tears. She wanted to know what is wrong that he is not embarrassed about exposing himself emotionally with a person he doesn't even know. She asked him to relax and she told him everything will be fine. She kept on saying that everything will be fine, whatever it is. After a while she felt that he has calmed down; she asked him what the matter is? Mukul was now a little embarrassed about crying on the phone and that too with someone who accidentally dialled his number.

He mustered up all the strength that was left in him and he apologized for his outburst. He waited with baited breath as to what would she say. She said it was okay, and she said she understood. There was a pregnant pause now between them. Both wanted to say something but nothing would come out. She wanted to tell him that she's sorry that she dialled his number and she is sorry that he was bothered because she got the wrong number. But somehow she ended up asking him, what is it that is bothering you and why did you break down like that.? Mukul was a bit taken aback with her sudden interest in his situation and he wanted to reply back that it's none of her business but he ended up saying that an incident has turned his life upside down and he blames himself for what has happened. He told her that he is consumed up totally in his guilt. His own voice seemed foreign to him and he was astonished as to why he said what he said to a girl who dialled a wrong number.

She was speechless for a few seconds, she was not anticipating this answer; she thought that he would reply with sarcasm or he would shout at her for prying into his life; but his answer came as a shock to her and she was trying to find the right words to reply to him. She told him not to let an incident jeopardize his whole life; she said that she is not aware about what has happened in his life but she knows for sure that he will overcome that. Life cannot stop; one incident cannot overpower us to such an extent. One has to find courage and fight back and one has to take a shot at life irrespective of what has happened. Life has never been easy, for anyone; nothing worth living for or for that matter dying for comes easy. One has to struggle everyday to make a life that we have imagined for ourselves. You do not get things on platter; you have to make your own platter. One cannot let one incident no matter how bad it is take over our whole being. A man is never defeated by people around him or emotions that surround him; he is defeated when he thinks that he is. It's all in the mind and if one wants sanity to prevail in life, one has to control mind. Every battle is first won in the mind and then in reality; so never let your mind feel that it's defeated.

She paused after this and gave him time to sink in everything that she has just said. Mukul was dumbfounded; he just did not know how to react. The girl on the other hand was a stranger and yet everything that she said made sense to him and he was rendered speechless because never in his entire life has anyone been so empathetic to him and so giving in terms of wisdom or kindness. His entire being was shaking vigorously and the cloud that has engulfed him was beginning to fade and to him her words were making sense; but still he was unable to shake off the thought of killing himself.

Again after an interminable silence he gathered up his strength and told her that his childhood has not been an easy one; he was adopted and his adoptive parents were too demanding about everything. They wanted him to excel in studies, sports, arts, theatre and they never ever cared for his opinions; all they did his entire life was to mould him the way they were; they never bothered even to ask him what was it that he wanted from life. What were his ambitions and what made him happy. He lived his life by the rules they made and then all of a sudden they were gone; they left him helpless and powerless. To the world he was a highly accomplished person but he knew deep down that he was a broken man and nothing could ever fix him or heal his wounds. But then after all there was a silver lining in the sky and it came in the form of Maya. Maya became the epicentre of his world and she gave a new meaning to his life and his entire being. He couldn't have asked for more from god. All his days used to be filled with love, laugh and happiness. Maya always made everyone happy around her and everyone in return showered her with love. She helped him heal his wounds and she was the one who helped him rediscover himself. Mukul paused, and he smiled; despite the condition he was in right now, the mere thought of Maya and her dazzling garrulous laughter and her shiny eyes, made him smile and for a mere second he felt the heavy weight that he has been carrying around for a while lift a little.

He could feel the warm tears rolling down his eyes but he did nothing to stop them. He continued. She was listening with apt attention and she wanted to know what happened that he has again engulfed himself in gloom. Mukul told her that happiness in his life was short lived and that day arrived when he again fell into that chasm which was so deep that there was no way out. He and Maya had gone out for a play and it was almost 1 when they were returning home. Mukul took a short-cut to reach home early, Maya was against it as she kept saying that the road is deserted and if anything happens to the car the help might be far away. But somewhere he was adamant and he eventually took the turn for the short cut. They had just gone some 600 meters when all of a sudden their car collided with another car that was on the wrong side and the collision was head on. The impact of the collision was so much that he was thrown out of the car and his head was hit by a boulder and he was left unconscious. Maybe he said that one can call it an unfortunate fate that the people who were driving on the wrong side were not affected by the accident and they fled away from the spot; leaving him and Maya in pain.

It was in the morning that a passerby noticed them and he called for the police. After that life went into a daze. They were taken to the hospital, he was fine expect for a slight injury on his head by the boulder but Maya was injured badly in the accident and now she was fighting for her life. Seeing her in pain crushed him and he just felt that somewhere that ghastly accident took away his soul. He was now repenting that why he never heeded to her advice. But now there was no point in regretting. Eventually Maya succumbed to her injuries and she passed away hours after she was admitted to the hospital.

It has been a month since all that happened and now he has no will to live. He blames himself for what happened that night, and he cannot forgive himself. It took her a while to grasp in the magnanimity of his words, his life and what happened to him and the girl he loved more than anything in the world. She was struggling to find the right words to console him and nothing was coming to mind. It was all a little too overwhelming to sink in and she totally understood his mental turmoil; but still that was no reason to end one's life.

She told him to take it easy. She reminded him that he wanted to be a strong person; he detested being weak, emotionally or otherwise. She reminded him that this is the time that he will have to prove that he is capable of handling situations and he is capable of fighting back whatever life has to throw at him. This is the moment that he will have to prove himself to the world that he is not an emotional coward and he can handle situations and he will have to muster up all the strength that he has to fight for his love. She argued with him, that how can he give up so easily for that one person who was his world. How can he disappoint her or her love?

Mukul felt his whole being shook up by her words; in his own worries and his own turmoil he has completely overlooked that he has to fight for Maya. Her words made sense to him. The fog of apprehensions, fear and dilemma was now beginning to descend and he could see a flicker of light, which would keep him alive and would give him strength to fight for the woman he loved more than anyone or anything in the world. All his life he has complained that he lacked strength to fight back the struggles and injustices thrown at him and now when he has a chance to prove himself, he is backing off and taking an easy way out. Her words made sense that only a cowardly mind could contemplate an act of suicide.

She felt relieved that this chance dialling of a wrong number, saved his life; at-least she was sure that she made sense in what she told him and she was sure that he understood. His feelings were apparent in his voice and she could sense that his gloom has lifted. She heaved a sigh of relief. She was smiling that she could least do this for a strange man.

He was fumbling with words to thank her, that call has been a life saviour and he just didn't know how to thank her. He said thank you a million times to her and when he was just on the verge of asking her, her name the call got disconnected. Mukul was shaking, he so wanted to meet her in person and thank her but the call just dropped suddenly the way it came.

He got up and threw his drink down the drain and he walked out into the terrace and he just stood still in the rain thinking how one call changed him, changed his take on life. How he wanted to thank that girl, but he was certain now that she called him because it was meant to be and he was certain that someday, maybe someday their paths will cross again and till then he will fight back for himself and Maya.

=()=

Gold Bangles

Part I

The constant beeping of the monitors above Ma was an indication that things were slightly in control. My eyes were just fixated on those monitors; even a slight change in them sent shivers down my spine and it used to consume me with a feeling of dread mingled with emptiness. Baba, and Suhasini, my elder sister, offered that they would stay here at the hospital and I could take a break; but no, that was not possible, I felt that if I left hospital Ma would die. I knew Ma was dying, and there was no way we could have saved her. But, then you can never ever think of the person you have loved the most in the world, and the person who has given you unconditional love, no matter what, of dying. It would be a blasphemous thought.

I took Ma's fragile hand in mine and closed my eyes. I travelled back in time, when we didn't have much. Still we were happy. Ma always used to say that we should not compare happiness to material things, but we were kids and we wanted everything that we couldn't get. You cannot expect a lot of profound wisdom from kids. Well, ours was a small family, just the four of us - Ma, Baba, Suhasini and me. Baba had a small clerical job and making ends meet in a big city, even in the 70's, was a bit difficult. Even though my parents had to struggle to make things work, they tried give us everything that was in their reach. We were educated at an English medium school, were enrolled for some sports classes that Ma used say were good for us, and even those extra dance classes, which Suhasini and me never ever liked. Our parents did everything that they could to provide me and Suhas (she was fondly called that) for us to have a better life. I still recall, Ma only had two sarees for some special occasions, and she never complained. All she wanted was us to have everything.

Ma always used to write in her diary at night, no matter what. And, she never allowed anyone to ever touch her dairy. She always said that it's a part of her life which she doesn't want to share. As a kid, her diary used to hold a special attraction for me, and more so because it was forbidden to touch. I still remember, it was on a rainy afternoon, when Ma was away for some errand, and I knew that she won't be back for at least an hour or more. I climbed up to her cupboard and grabbed her diary. The moment I started reading it, I came across a very different person my Ma was. Like, I never knew she was so fond of writing poetry, that as a young girl she used to imagine herself as a poetess. On the next page, she wrote that her mother scolded her for having dreams like that, as she used think that poor like them didn't have any right to dream as their life was only subjected to making ends meet. How unfair that statement must have been for my Ma, who was actually a talented poetess. I read some of her works in the dairy and I was impressed. Ma wrote that she buried her dreams the day she got married, and readied herself for a life that lay ahead of her which only promised her struggle. But, she vowed in her diary that she would never ever tell her girls to bury their dreams or never to dream. She always kept true to her vow. As far as I can remember, she always encouraged us to dream no matter what. She wrote that she would do her best to give us a life that would allow us to dream and maybe someday fulfil them too. Reading further, I realized that Ma never ever had any material wishes in her life, expect for just one thing. She wrote that she never aspired for any worldly pleasures, but she just had this one secret desire of having a gold bangle. Even when she got married, neither my grandparents have any gold jewellery to give to their daughter, nor could Baba afford any back then. Somewhere, she knew that bringing up two daughters and educating them would not leave her with this luxury of buying a gold bangle. So, as she had to bury that little wish for good. The part where she wrote about the gold bangle was a little smudged; maybe she must have cried writing that. A tear rolled down my eyes thinking of my Ma, who was so selfless. Her love for us was so much, that she sacrificed her life, and even her little desires for us. I closed her diary and kept it back in the place where it was, but that afternoon doubled my respect for my mother.

I all of a sudden woke up from my memory ridden slumber, and I ran towards the reception area. I called up my sister and Baba, and asked to come to the hospital as I told them that I have some very urgent work to attend to, and I would need them both with Ma for a while. The moment Baba and Suhasini arrived I left.

Part II

Ma was awake when I got back. She smiled at me weakly and instructed me to come and sit by her side. I sat beside her, and while she looked the other way trying to listen to what Baba was saying, I slipped something on her hands. A little taken by the gesture she looked at me quizzically. I was so overwhelmed with emotions that I couldn't speak so I just indicated her through my eyes to look at her hands. She looked at it, and she just kept looking at it while tears flooded her eyes. I really don't know how and when I got so busy in life, that I completely forgot about Ma's diary and the vow that I made to myself that day, that the day I would be in a position to fulfil her desire, I would make it my first priority. But, somewhere in my career I just forgot all about it. How selfish that was on my part; even now I cannot bring to forgive myself for that.

Ma passed away four days after that. But I will never forget that look of satisfaction and gratitude in her eyes for me. She flaunted those gold bangles to everyone in the hospital, and every time someone used to praise them, she would look at me and say "My daughter got this for me, aren't they the prettiest you have ever seen..?" Nothing in the whole world could have compared to her beatific smile, and an expression of pride in her eyes.

=()=

A Mystery Called Love

Love is an unsolved mystery,
A beautiful pandora box of mysteries.
Love has its ups and downs,
Makes you listen to its sweet sounds.
Love is true, Love is real,
Love is sweet, Love is surreal.
Love brings smile, Love brings tears,
Love makes you conquer all your fears.
Love makes you do crazy things,
It washes away all your sins.
So fall in love and go crazy,
Go! Find your love; Don't be lazy.

A Perfect World

She had a dream of a perfect world; where
there was love and only love for all.
Life would be a bed of roses in her perfect world;
where no struggle would go unacknowledged
and justice would be for all.
Pretensions would be barred in her perfect world;
showing true colors would be mandatory for all.
The sun would never set over the
happiness of the perfect world.
Ahh!! She really wishes she sees this perfect world!!

Been Around The World

I have known people, I have been to places,
Not in my dreams but in my mind,
I have been to the moon with Neil Armstrong,
and I have seen the beauty of stars.
So, do you wonder, how did I see so much?
Well, I have seen the world in my books.

I met Gandhi and I met Churchill,
I met Tagore and I met Keats,
I sang with Sinatra and played a little with Beethoven.
Would you ask me how?
Well, I have seen the world in my books.

I witnessed the ghastly woes and sufferings at Auschwitz,
And I cried with Anne Frank in her silent sufferings.
Would you ask me how?
Well, I have seen the world in my books.

I saw the determination of Rani of Jhansi,
I saw the courage of brave Indian soldiers,
I witnessed the battle for our motherland in 1857,
And I sadly saw the English crush us in 1857.
Would you ask me how?
Well, I have seen the world in my books.

I have been there when the Prince kissed Snow-white,
I was there when the little bird
Shuktugun took its first flight.
Would you ask me how?
Well, I have seen the world in my books.

I have been on the ship with Robinson Crusoe,
I also wandered with Huckleberry Finn,
I kissed Tom Sawyer and hugged the gin from Aladdin.
Would you ask me how?
Well, I have seen the world in my books.

Belief

People believe in God but not in humanity.
People believe in sex but not in love.
People believe in friendship but not in loyalty.
People believe in spirits but not in angels.
People believe in laughter but not in happiness.
People believe in character but not in morals.
People believe in life but not in living.
People believe in receiving but not in giving.
People believe in passion but not in compassion.
People believe in chatter but not in silence.
People believe in togetherness but not in solitude.
People believe in grudge but not in forgiveness.
People believe in heart but not in inner soul.

Daddy Where Are You?

She used to ask her Ma, where's daddy gone?
Her Ma kept saying he is gone for long.
Years passed by; but her daddy never came by.
She kept wondering where is he?
Does this lock have a key?
Then one day when her Ma went out; the little girl
thought this is the best time to clear her doubt.
She opened the mysterious trunk in her mother's room,
She was in for a gloom.
She saw the picture of a most perfect man,
She could make out the resemblance, yes she can.
Behind the picture some words were scribbled,
She read that and was in tears, her
daddy was dead all these years.
Her Ma kept him alive because she didn't
want her little girl to be sad.
So she let her search for him everywhere.
Truth was hidden to shield the little girl from sadness.
All her Ma wanted was to save her little
girl some emotional madness.

How Time Flies

It was just yesterday that I used to
play in my Papa's backyard,
Ahh!! How time flies.
It was just yesterday that I used to pack
my bags and hop to school,
Ahh! How time flies.
It was just yesterday that I used to play
hide and seek with my friends,
Ahh!! How time flies.
It was just yesterday that even a small box of
crayons used to be a treasured thing,
Ahh!! How time flies.
It was just yesterday that I was an uncomplicated human
being with no expectations from life but just happiness,
Ahh!! How time flies.
It was just yesterday that fights used to get settled in
minutes unlike now when we don't want to let it go,
Ahh!! How time flies.
It was just yesterday that happiness was not
an aspiration but a constant reality,
Ahh!! How time flies.
It was just yesterday that I wanted to grow up fast
and be an adult but now I really want to go back in
time and be that carefree little girl I used to be,
Ahh!! I wish time flies back.

I Am Not A Virgin

I am not a virgin, maybe it is my sin,
Because perfection was supposed to be my twin.
Losing virginity sadly is a crime,
Don't you think that change is required high time?
I lost it at my own will,
And I do not need the world's moral grill.
Why can't I be a mistress of my own life?
Is it necessary to hold a woman against this barbaric strife?
Time is shouting at its highest decibel,
World really needs to be slightly ethical.
If a man can have sex for pleasure,
Then why is a woman questioned for the same measure?
Equality should be the order of the day,
Let's keep conventional qualms at bay.
I am not a virgin, maybe it is my sin,
Because perfection was supposed to be my twin.

I'm Flawed

Yes I'm flawed. And I'm not ashamed to admit that.
I'm jealous sometimes and I'm also vengeful many a
times and some days I'm a total condescending brat.
I'm prone to most common human failings and
no I have no qualms in accepting that.
Sometimes I cannot control my emotions for
the sake of it and I vent out my anger and you
know what I'm not embarrassed about that.
Sometimes I'm rude and sometimes I'm crude.
Sometimes I'm the gentlest girl you have ever met. You
may call me strange; I have no problem with that.
I have PMS and I do have horrible mood swings. One
moment I'll be sweet as a sugar and the other moment I
might be as bitter as a quinine; and no I have no pride in
that but I'm original and not a pretender which is a fact.
I have a mind of my own and yes sometimes I am
prejudiced too. I believe in speaking my heart
out and I hate bolting emotions for the sake of
peace. Maybe I'm not that mushy fairytale girl you
imagined me to be but then who cares for that.
This is my life and I am going to live it to the fullest
with my flaws intact. I don't care if the world likes me or
not; so far the world has been bitter to people who speak
their heart out and I'm just one more straw in that hat.

I live life by my own rules, even though they are unrealistic sometimes and I care to hoots for the society and once again I have no repentance for that. Yes I'm flawed. And I'm not ashamed to admit that.

In The Sky

He was in the air he felt as if he could
stretch his hands and touch the sky.
He thought how beautiful this feeling is of
being in the air, maybe for sometime but you
could leave your earthly worries there and hug
the openness of the skies and beyond.
He could see the birds flying there with
him; he envied their power to fly.
He flew back in time when he was a little boy who also
wanted to be a bird, when asked why? He would always
answer that how beautiful it is to have the freedom to fly
and go anywhere your heart wants no strings attached.
In the skies for even sometime he could
keep his worries at bay and smile.
Life he thought from up here looks so trivial, the
problems seem meaningless; maybe because the sky
is so vast that for some moments it envelopes your
troubles in its hugeness and lets you breathe free.
Today while flying he saw a troubled vision of his long
dead father and it left him with a feeling of dread.
He has always seen his father in dreams, he
so adored him and when his father died he left
a vacuum which no one ever could fill.
The vision of his father was telling him to go
back but he in his flying furore he ignored
the warning and flew even high up.

He wanted to see the world of angels he has read
about in the books; he wanted the world to see
how he conquered the indomitable skies.
Suddenly he lost control, no matter what he
did he kept going down and further down.
When he was descending down at a scary pace,
in that wild moment of fear his life rolled past his
eyes in a blurry kaleidoscope of memories from the
past. He wanted to hold on to something to save
himself the fall, he wanted to rectify the mistakes
that he had made but now there was no time left.
He hit the ground and his plane caught fire.
He got out of it and with sad remorseful eyes he saw
his own charred self being carried by his grieving
mother. He wanted to touch her and tell her that he
is still here but now he was lost in a labyrinth and
there was no way out of it. He sighed and sat under
the tree and waited for the agony of death to relive
him forever and take him to the higher plains.

*** Dedicated to Sanjay Gandhi.*

Karna

I was looking at the portrait of a hero, a warrior,
His built was stoic, he exhumed confidence,
But still there in his eyes I saw a forlorn look,
I saw those big beautiful eyes brimming
with sadness and irony.

It felt as if he was hurt,
But he was trying hard to conceal the hurt,
He wore a look of dejection from the
world on his handsome face,
Even amidst the crowd he looked lost and
his sad eyes were staring in space.

Looking at him it seemed that his
entire life has been a misery,
There was no need for him to tell his story,
His eyes spoke volumes about the irony that his life was,
Known as the maverick around the world,
for his own self he had nothing at all.

I wanted to reach out to that man with
those sad eyes in the picture,
I wanted to tell him that I am there,
It seems he wanted to hear those words,
That said that no matter what I am there
and you shall not be alone anymore.

He was the bravest of them all,
But still it seemed he was the most vulnerable of all,
If I had powers to rewrite his destiny,
I would have given him justice, because
that was missing for this hero's life.

Message From A Soul

I am a spirit and I don't have a name,
Roaming around in the night is my game.
It has been years since I died,
It made me sad when I saw my mother, who cried.
I tried to wipe away her tears,
But now I wasn't so near.
One moment I was alive,
Another moment it was all a lie.
If you are born you are to die,
In between you live, laugh, love and cry.
The misery of a spirit is it can see loved ones in pain,
But it cannot go and soothe their aching
hearts as it held by the deathly chains.
You have nothing with you but your
good deeds and regrets,
Spirit world is unforgiving for people with emotional debts.
You just wait in agony every day,
Keeping aside your anticipation for a new life at bay.
I plead to god, please let me stay with you,
Because the world down there is just, oh!! so blue.
I am happy in the form I roam,
Only this way I can call the whole world my home.
Till you live just love and smile,
After then begins your journey of miles and miles.

<u>One Day</u>

I wish I could I could live one day without compulsions.
I wish I could live one day without pretence.
I wish I could live one day without a watch.
I wish I could live one day without idiosyncrasies.
I wish I could live one day without
worrying about the next day.
I wish I could live one day without
anything to regret about.
I wish I could live one day without money.
I wish I could live one day without anger.
I wish I could live one day without a facade.
I wish I could live one day without prejudices.
I wish I could live one day as if it
was the last day of my life.
I wish to live that one day once in my
life. Where, I'll be "Me".
There won't be any pretence, there won't be any wall
between me and the world, there would be just "Me".

Poker Face Man

As a child I understood a fact that world
doesn't care for your feelings,
Earlier in life I learned to keep my emotions
inside me because there is no use revealing.
I am a poker face man.

Many a times I was called a man with no heart,
Well, I did not care for that as you know
I mastered for years for that part.
I am a poker face man.

I was called an enigma maybe hard to understand,
I was happy so far because life was
exactly the way I planned.
I am a poker face man.

Revealing you feelings makes you
vulnerable that I knew for sure,
I was not that strong to deal with the heart ache it brought
and so I kept my feelings to myself safe and secure.
I am a poker face man.

It was not an act of bravery on my part
to have kept my feelings hidden,
Rather it was an act of saving myself from falling
apart as that in my world was forbidden.
I am a poker face man.

I have been called a coward, I have
been named a weakling,
But for me that was the only way I could
have saved my soul from weeping.
Yes I am a poker face man.

Rosary Beads

She saw the casket being buried in the ground.
With it went her childhood, her first love, her memories
of life that now lay buried and with it went her security
and her pillar of strength. With it went her Mother
whom she loved more than anything in the world.
She wanted to cry, she wanted to shout but noting
came out of her mouth. It felt as if the words were
frozen inside her. She felt emotionally paralysed.
She went numb mentally. She didn't know how to react.
Now the only remainder of her Mother
was her rosary beads.
She was clinging to those rosary beads as
if it would bring back her Mother.
The softness of the rosary beads reminded her of her
Mother's loving hands. It still smelt of her Mother.
Those rosary beads gave her the security and
warmth she was craving for. It wasn't her mother
but it had been her mother's dearest possession.
Her Mother has always held it close to her heart and
now she was clinging to them for some miracle to
happen. She was now desperately clinging to them
because she wanted it to bring back her Mother.
But sadly her mother was gone and all she
was left with was those rosary beads!

Waiting

Her eyes were fixated on the door; with
waiting and just waiting for him everyday
her heart was now emotionally sore.
She closed her eyes and travelled back in
time; she had just given birth to a cherubic
baby boy and oh! He was so divine.
He filled her world with his happy smiles and love;
for her he was a little angel sent from up above.
She remembered spending sleepless nights
for him when he was sick; making him feel
all well, was always her cherished feat.
He grew up fast into a young man of confidence;
now only his ambition was in his life a constant.
He got busier and busier in life; somewhere
she sadly thought it deepened between them
the now so ever present constant rife.
She introspected where she went wrong; but the
answer to her question was gone and she thought
living with this pain was now lifelong.
She never wanted much from him but just some
time; she also understood that he has dreams to
chase and fulfil them as he is still in his prime.

She has been waiting in this hospital bed
for now so long, that sometimes she feels
as if this is where she truly belongs.
Her heart was tired now of waiting for him
every single day; just for her son she was
even keeping her angels of death at bay.
She said aloud that she is his mother and she
will forgive him as he is her only child; the mere
thought of him even in her pain made her smile.
The monitor screen now showed a flat line; she died
waiting for her only son. Even the angels cried for a selfless
mother when they saw her enter the heavenly shrine.

Was It Time To Say Goodbye?

Stomp, Stomp, Stomp.
They stomped in the school; the intention was not good,
They were bad, they were sinister.
They were the monsters we read in books but in
contrast to them even the monsters looked good.
We were unaware of the tragic end we would meet,
Never ever anyone would have thought
this too is a way death greets.
Our tiny hearts knew no bad existed in the world and there
came these men who thrashed our beliefs in just one shot.
We wondered what our fault was. We
wondered was it time to say goodbye?

We were told children are next to gods,
But what unfolded in front of us was very odd.
We were taught to love even the tiniest of microorganisms,
As life is too short to waste in hating anyone.
And there came these men, who looked so
incapable of loving the creatures of god,
We wondered what our fault was. We
wondered was it time to say goodbye.

138

We were pretty sure even the gods in heaven
would have shuddered at the sight down below,
The gods must have wondered where they went wrong
when they created the humans with those ghastly thoughts.
They were monsters in a human's garb,
God must have thought these are the
ones who defame humanity.
These are the ones who have no sanity.

Children are the dreams and hope of future,
And we are supposed to love them and nurture.
But some misguided beings made a vendetta
and trampled harshly upon the little ones,
There tiny hearts and bodies were
full of those bullet wounds.
Again we wondered what our fault was. We
wondered was it time say goodbye.

Children are the future a country depends on; children are our hopes and dreams; let's protect them and make them believe that world is a safer place. Let us pledge that we will never ever December 16 repeat it. That day is a black mark on humans; I guess even animals have better morals than we all do. Let us make our children feel safe again. Let us instil humanity again.

The poem is my tribute to the little ones who passed way before their time. May their souls rest in peace and may the culprits be brought down to justice.

=()=

What Have You Done?

On a cold wintry morning, I was sitting on my window sill,
When from suddenly nowhere came a little
girl and she stood in front of me.
She looked me in the eye and asked
"What have you done to yourself".
I was dumbstruck, I kept looking at her piercing
eyes and between us the time stood still.

She came and sat beside me, and in my mind
I was still questioning her sheer identity,
She took my hand and said "You promised
something to yourself when you were a kid".
I had no answer to her statement, because it
was a long long time ago in the past,
She said clean the cobwebs and dwell in the memories
of that little girl who is now a forgotten entity.

I closed my eyes tightly to escape to my buried
memories; I searched for that little girl who
always dreamed to reach for the stars,
I found her in the darkest corners of my mind,
where she sat still crying for the lost promise.
When I confronted the crying little girl I
was shocked, she was the same the little girl
who now stood in front of me, was ME,

I in my haste and twisted feelings couldn't even
recognize my own self; I thought was I so scarred?

As a little girl I was full of life and big dreams, life was
going to be a happy roller coaster ride back then,
But somehow the dreams of childhood got
buried in the realities of adulthood.
I forgot how I promised myself as a little girl to be
always happy and no matter what always strong,
And now here I am confronted by my own self and I ask
myself can I be that brave dreamy girl once again?

That little girl sitting with me on the window
sill gave me an epiphany to dwell in,
She looked me in the eye and said "World
is perishable, dreams die people die but
my dear never ever let your soul die".
She continued "Do not let a moment of weakness
make you believe you are defeated because life is not
about defeats it's about your victory over them",
She patted my hand and walked into the mist she came
from and I sat looking at her disappear again and thinking
that it's time to recollect myself and recover from within.

Winds Of Time

Oh the winds of time,
Take me to a place where the world is still a pretty rhyme.
A place where there's only love and that's truly divine.
Oh the winds of time!

Oh the winds of time,
Let me embrace the beauty of nature
that no words could define.
Take me to a world that is not yours
or mine but ours to design.
Oh the winds of time!

Oh the winds of time,
Let this world be one in true sense as it was destined.
A world where every human soul is a worthy shrine.
Oh the winds of time!

Oh the winds of time,
Please make my dream of a beautiful world come true.
As the world we live in today is oh so blue.
Oh the winds of time, Oh the winds of time!

Time

We never realize how quickly the years pass by,
But it takes eternity for minutes to tick by.
When we are happy time flies like
a kite without the thread,
But when we are down in the dumps every
single second is an agonizing dread.
Sometimes I wonder and ask the creator why
you divided our life in twenty four hours,
Why did you not bestow upon us some
of your magical powers?
Life would have been a smooth sailing ship if
there was no clock ticking by all the time,
There would have been no rush and everyone's
life would have been a sweet rhyme.
Time is the biggest culprit in the game of life,
It sometimes rips open your life apart like a piercing knife.
Please make time disappear,
And life would be happy all around the year.

Whiny Humans!

When we have all the wealth we aspired for,
We yearn for the health that was lost
accumulating the wealth.
Whiny humans whiny humans!
When we have happiness that we so wished for,
We yearn for green pastures that go beyond us.
Whiny humans whiny humans!
When we get the opportunity we always looked for,
We yearn for another one and let go off the one we got.
Whiny Humans whiny humans!
When all our lives we wait for a perfect ending of life,
But alas when it comes, we cling to
life begging some more time.
Whiny humans whiny humans!
When we are contented, we want more contentment.
When we have abundance of wealth,
we want more opulence.
When we have al l the happiness in the
world, we aspire for euphoria.
When we have a reason to smile, we want laughter.
No matter what we have it will always be less.
No matter how much god gives us,
we will always want more.
Whiny humans whiny humans!

Her Life

She was an orphan, she roamed around
the town all alone and scared.
She had no one to show that she was emotionally impaired.
Life was not easy being all alone,
In darkness of her pain she would let out a moan.
The only person who cared was god
But to her sometimes even he was flawed.
But her patience never gave away
She kept alive her hope every day.
Life was never meant to be easy had said her dad
Remembering him made her sad.
She took a dive back in time
When her life was a melodious rhyme.
She was a happy little girl with only love around her
Her father made only happiness surround her.
Suddenly the perfect world vanished into thin air
And to her this was not at all fair.
She yearned for the happy days to come
As she wanted to be with her favourite chum.
Hope has kept her alive all along
And she knew that for better days she has to stay strong.
God loves her and he will prove it
Because she faithfully believes in his holy spirit.